PRAIRIE PASSAGE

I&M Canal and State Trail, Gebhard Woods State Park, Morris.

PRAIRIE PASSAGE

The Illinois and Michigan Canal Corridor

Photographs by

EDWARD RANNEY

Prologue by

TONY HISS

Essays by

EMILY J. HARRIS

Epilogue by

WILLIAM LEAST HEAT-MOON

UNIVERSITY OF ILLINOIS PRESS *Urbana and Chicago*

CANAL CORRIDOR ASSOCIATION

Manufactured in the United States of America
1 2 3 4 5 C P 5 4 3 2 1

This book is printed on acid-free paper.
Designed by Eleanor Caponigro
Duotone negatives made by Thomas Palmer
Printed by Hull Printing
Bound by Roswell Bookbinding

LIBRARY OF CONGRESS
CATALOGING-IN-PUBLICATION DATA
Ranney, Edward.
Prairie Passage : the Illinois and Michigan Canal corridor / photographs by Edward Ranney ; prologue by Tony Hiss ; essays by Emily J. Harris ; epilogue by William Least Heat-Moon.
p. cm.
Includes bibliographical references (p.).
ISBN 0–252–02411–7 (acid-free paper)
ISBN 0–252–06714–2 (pbk. : acid-free paper)
1. Illinois and Michigan Canal National Heritage Corridor (Ill.)—Pictorial works. 2. Illinois and Michigan Canal National Heritage Corridor (Ill.)—Descriptions and travel. 3. Illinois and Michigan Canal National Heritage Corridor (Ill.)—History, Local.
I. Harris, Emily. II. title.
F547. I13R36 1998
977.3'2—DDC21 98–8906
CIP

The Edward Ranney
photographs in this book
are dedicated to the memory of
Richard H. Bliss (1920–90) and
Edward L. Ryerson (1886–1971).

CONTENTS

ACKNOWLEDGMENTS

This project was initially made possible in part by grants from the Illinois Humanities Council, the National Endowment for the Humanities, and the Illinois General Assembly. These grants funded Edward Ranney's collaboration with scholars in the humanities as he photographed the Illinois and Michigan Canal National Heritage Corridor and researched the region's photographic record. They also supported the participation of William Least Heat-Moon and Tony Hiss. Other early donors included the Donnelley Foundation, the Thomas E. II and Barbara C. Donnelley Family Fund; the Graham Foundation for Advanced Studies in the Arts; and the Gaylord and Dorothy Donnelley Foundation.

In 1996, thanks to the leadership of Speaker of the House Lee Daniels, the state of Illinois made a major grant through the Illinois Historic Preservation Agency to underwrite *Prairie Passage* in recognition of the I&M Canal sesquicentennial celebration. Matching funds were contributed by Paul Carus II, the Elizabeth Cheney Foundation, Strachan Donnelley, the John D. and Catherine T. MacArthur Foundation, Morton International, and Victoria and George Ranney Jr.

Like all projects in the Illinois and Michigan Canal National Heritage Corridor, this publication is the result of extensive collaboration. The following are among the many people and organizations who have provided support and assistance.

A number of scholars have guided this project from its inception, providing the foundation for understanding the canal region and, literally, acting as guides for the photographer. They include James Brown, Michael P. Conzen, Ted Karamanski, John Lamb, and Dominic Pacyga. George Bullwinkel and Lewis University (thanks to its president, Br. James Gaffney) provided planes for the aerial photography.

Many others provided access to specific sites and offered valuable background information, including Dan Bell, Char Giardina, Fran Harty, and Judy Schoenenberger of the Illinois Department of Natural Resources; David Bielenberg and Carl Kueltzo of the Metropolitan Water Reclamation District; Jim DaRosa of the Lockport Township

Park District; Stephen Aultz and Jean Knight of the Forest Preserve District of Will County; M. Blouke and Inga Carus at Carus Chemical Corporation; Dale Dunn at the Chicago River Lock; Marvin Lauterjung of Illinois Power; Rick Rimbo at UnoVen (now Citgo); Brian Marsden and Mike Lawbaugh at Acme Steel Company; and Dennis Engeleart at Mobil Oil Corporation.

A number of public forums were held during the research process, and the Canal Corridor Association appreciated the cosponsorship of the Heritage Corridor Visitors Bureau and the I&M Canal National Heritage Corridor Civic Center Authority of Cook County, as well as the participation of the Friends of the I&M Canal and the Illinois and Michigan Canal National Heritage Corridor Commission. Speakers whose input is reflected in this book include Michael Conzen, Edmund B. Thornton, Debbie Steffes, Tom Alves, John Husar, and Stan Johnson.

Numerous libraries and archives were searched for photographic and other visual material, and staff there could not have been more helpful. We particularly appreciate the assistance of the Blue Island Historical Society, Chicago Historical Society, East Side Historical Society, George Eastman House, La Salle County Historical Society, La Salle Public Library, Lemont Historical Society, Lewis University Canal Collection, Library of Congress, Morris Public Library, Newberry Library, St. Bede's Academy, and Peru Public Library. The Metropolitan Water Reclamation District of Greater Chicago generously made their glass-plate negatives available for reprinting, as did private collectors Peter Loveland of Maze Lumber and P. H. Ogren. We are also indebted to the following private collectors who were generous with their time, knowledge, photographs, postcards, paintings, illustrations, and maps: Gerald W. Adelmann, Alwin Carus, Dorothy Clemens, James Jensen, Barry MacLean, Ruth Packham, David R. Phillips/Chicago Architectural Photographing Co., Robert E. Sterling, Edmund Thornton, and Tom Willcockson.

Canal Corridor Association staff and consultants have assisted with this project over the years, and we particularly appreciate the contributions of Gerald W. Adelmann, Vince Michael, Laurie Scott, Alan Teller, Simona Mkrtschjan, Alf Siewers, and Christine Esposito. Association officers Barbara C. Donnelley, Philip W. Hummer, and John T. Trutter provided extraordinary board-level leadership for the project. Victoria and George Ranney Jr. contributed their counsel and their editorial and fund-raising talents in addition to their own generous support. *Prairie Passage* would not have achieved its final form without their involvement.

The Illinois State Museum is the cosponsor of the exhibits that will accompany this book, and its director, R. Bruce McMillan, has been extremely helpful throughout the project, as have Kent Smith and Jim Zimmer. Venues include the Chicago Cultural Center, thanks to the City of Chicago Department of Cultural Affairs, the Illinois State Museum Gallery in Lockport, and the Illinois State Museum in Springfield.

We are indebted to Richard L. Wentworth, director and editor in chief of the University of Illinois Press, for his commitment to publish *Prairie Passage* and to Theresa L. Sears, for her invaluable editing.

The design and structure of *Prairie Passage*, as well as the title, were created by Eleanor Morris Caponigro, whose overseeing of all aspects of production has ensured the standards of excellence for which her work is known. We are deeply appreciative of her participation.

Celebrating the
Sesquicentennial of the Illinois and Michigan Canal and
the Fifteenth Anniversary of the Illinois and Michigan Canal
National Heritage Corridor

1. *I&M Canal Lock No. 12, west of Ottawa.*

PROLOGUE

An Eye to See and a Heart to Enjoy

TONY HISS

TAKING THE LONG VIEW

Although the exceptional photographs in *Prairie Passage* very specifically survey one extraordinary area in America – an undulating line of landscapes and waterscapes that stretches southwest from Lake Michigan and through Chicago for more than a hundred miles, this beautiful book also represents the coming of age of an increasingly important national experiment. Across the country, hundreds of towns, cities, and regions are trying to discover if it's possible to renew America by settling down and appreciating it.

In northern Illinois and wherever it's been taking root, this process has to do with seeing afresh the places where we live and work. It leads to a new kind of positive bookkeeping for places, as people set up and get the feeling for an accounting system that turns our customary thinking about assets upside down and inside out. The new assumptions are: wherever you are and whatever's been going on about you, almost any existing landscape or community has value it can recapture and build on, which means that every new project can start off in the black, with a positive balance in its ledger. Furthermore, in looking ahead, this system of evaluating places always takes the long view, so it's forethoughtful about compounding their value over the course of a generation, even when there's an immediate need to be eager for near-term gains.

As the photographs in *Prairie Passage* so meticulously and elegantly point out, time, as it flows through communities over decades and centuries, is not always an enemy and a thief, undermining worth, gnawing through value. Just as often, time is a ripener and a repairer, a force that can heal, scour, comfort, burnish, and recombine, sometimes restoring value, sometimes generating it. It's the sense of time, the sustainer, that suffuses the activities and accomplishments this book records. The recurring central image in *Prairie Passage* – the thread that sews its pages together – is its views of a narrow, shallow, long-abandoned, but now rediscovered nineteenth-century canal, the Illinois and Michigan, an alteration to the landscape that an ordinary listing of assets might

Plate 1. Eighteen-foot-wide stone locks enabled canal boats to navigate the 150-foot drop in elevation along the I&M Canal between Lake Michigan and the Illinois River. The original stone walls of the lock are pictured here.

ignore or discard altogether, seeing it only as a liability, ill used by time.

Take a first look: there are places where the I&M is nearly invisible, its banks either overgrown by an impenetrable tangle of brambles or overshadowed by looming storage tanks and sheds at the edge of large-scale modern industrial sites. Stretches of the I&M are so dry you couldn't even get a canoe through, and miles of the canal are missing altogether – filled in decades ago to make room for an elevated expressway.

Now take a second look, at the tremendously skillful, symmetrical simplicity of the stonework that lines the high, tight walls of the canal locks; at the way in which nineteenth-century engineers contrived the canal's course so that the I&M slips through the landscape with such tact, modesty, and neighborliness that communities are never compromised by its presence but only made more comfortable; at the canal's many confluences, the places where it cuts across or flows into another waterway, stream, river, or canal, and in so doing seems to come together with and lend its shape and dignity to a larger landscape.

The Illinois and Michigan Canal is one of those artifacts – planners call them "lovable objects" – that, even if they have no further story to tell, people can almost instinctively feel affectionate and protective toward them, thanks to their size and shape and workmanship. The integrity of such objects is not diminished by mere dilapidation. In landscape terms, this particular skinny old canal has yet another level of potential resonance, because it's a lovable object nested within the kind of place where awe can linger long, long after great natural events. An immense natural force shaped the larger area around the canal – what's there now is the remnant of a raging, icy torrent once as potent as Niagara or the Amazon and known to geologists as the Chicago Outlet Valley. Another name for it is the Prairie Passage.

The flat to gently rolling prairie landscape of northeastern Illinois, thought to be relatively featureless, is, geologists would say, a youthful place. This is land still springing upward after the weight of a mile-thick glacier has been removed. Twice, as the glacier retreated northward, its meltwater, confined in lakes far deeper than Lake Michigan, poured southwestward, carving cliffs, exposing rich mineral deposits, and leaving behind a deep, wide, unmistakable passageway through the prairie flatness. Each meltwater burst lasted about three thousand years, the last one ending perhaps three thousand years ago, long after Native Americans had come to think of Illinois as their homeland.

The I&M, sixty feet wide and six feet deep, and several marshy, shallow, many-islanded prairie rivers, broad and grassy, including the Des Plaines and the Illinois, wind their way down the middle of the Outlet Valley, which is two miles wide in

Figure 1. The broad Illinois River is formed west of Channahon by the confluence of the Des Plaines and Kankakee Rivers. The white line that runs between the canal and the river was the canal's towpath and is now the I&M Canal State Trail.

places and up to 150 feet deep. Cutting through the dry prairie upland, the outlet has a special character all its own, with wooded slopes and marshes and meadows of rare, wet prairie along the valley floor. The combined presence of the Illinois and Michigan Canal and the Chicago Outlet Valley has a federally bestowed, official name: the Illinois and Michigan Canal National Heritage Corridor.

If the imprint of time permeates *Prairie Passage*, the book also presents cases where time

Figure 2. A tiny parcel of land where the I&M Canal originated is all that is left of the canal in Chicago. Though located in a heavily industrialized area, the site, overlooking the Chicago River turning basin in the Bridgeport neighborhood, offers a safe haven every year for birds traveling the flyway along the Chicago Outlet Valley. The Canada geese seen here are feeding on melons from nearby fruit vendors. Other species using this riverfront site include the endangered black crowned night heron.

doesn't exist at all, or at least hasn't yet come into play. Looking through these pages, you'll here and there see pieces of communities that seem depreciated and diminished. You'll see just as many that, like the canalside towns of Lemont, Lockport, and Ottawa, are more than holding their own and even furiously regenerating – the awakening alongside the slumbering. There are places that in ten years have become unrecognizable, and places where a century has left as much impact as an hour. Often the time-accelerated sites and the no-time-elapsed spots are close neighbors: a beaver dam beside gigantic oil storage tanks; a car graveyard beside an ingenious new artificial waterfall that adds life-giving oxygen to a sluggish waterway.

These juxtapositions can be disorienting – until you begin to acquire a taste for them and are catapulted into a realization that the familiar is also the unexplored. In this light, renewing an area like the Prairie Passage becomes a matter of uncovering and re-evaluating and embracing again what is already there – as if Columbus had instead found his treasure at home in Spain. It's important to point out that this process isn't something that, either in the Prairie Passage or elsewhere, was developed as a theory and then, over time, worked out by scholars at universities. This is a battlefront discovery, seat-of-the-pants science, something that has emerged as an urgent response to a serious and sometimes dire situation where the immediate future of hard-pressed and rapidly changing communities hangs in the balance.

Can these communities survive? Should they? What have they got going for them? The same questions also echo through less care-worn communities across the nation, even in areas that seem to have successfully grounded themselves in the "three E's" – a shorthand way of saying that they enjoy vigorous economies, equitable communities, and healthy ecosystems. It's increasingly clear that no neighborhood and no region, whatever its accomplishments, can afford to think of itself as permanently immune from upheaval. There's too much going on for that to be so.

COUNTING BLESSINGS

According to recent projections, the more than 250 million Americans living today constitute a total only about two-thirds as large as the number of people who will be living here a century from now. Since the end of World War II, while our numbers have grown by about 60 percent, we've built what's sometimes called the "second America" – meaning that half the buildings in the country were built in the first 450 years after Columbus landed here, and the other half were built during the last 50 years. Everyone everywhere has been touched by that construction splurge. When you revisit the scenes of your own childhood, how much is even recog-

Figure 3. The site where the I&M Canal began has been used for many years for semitrailer parking, wholesale fruit and vegetable vending, a gas station, and a fried fish house. In honor of the I&M Canal's sesquicentennial in 1998, the Chicago Park District will create an interpretive park here, celebrating Chicago's history as a canal town and offering public access to the banks of the Chicago River (see pls. 17–18).

nizable today? And what about the scenes along the route you have to take between here and there?

How do we assess what we've accomplished? For instance, as we build more and build larger, how good a job are we doing of housing our highest aspirations? The "American experiment," our most daring undertaking, seeks to demonstrate that a full array of the world's talents and insights, of its ethnic groups, religions, and races, can create a new society and that, young or old, rich or poor, we can all live together in peace in the same country. But what parts of today's communities can serve as the cradles that might nurture such hopes?

In earlier decades, many redevelopment campaigns had one barometer for success: job growth. But re-exploring and rediscovering the value of a

Figure 4. The I&M Canal was once lined by tollhouses like this one in Ottawa, locktenders' houses, grain elevators, and factories, few of which survive. Tolls collected on the I&M paid off Illinois's $6.4 million canal debt by 1871.

place has to do with thinking not only about jobs – not about any one thing at all – but instead about the deeply entwined relationship between the prosperity of a place and all the other ways it affects people's lives. It's rather like inventory taking, counting up a community's blessings the way Audubon Society volunteers fan out every winter to conduct their "Christmas count" of the birds of North America. But taking stock in this way turns out to be a subtler business than it might appear, because it involves looking around with several sets of eyes at once.

You seek out the bright qualities and pleasures available that could nourish people and sustain their hopes – places for contemplation and places for conviviality; the right spots for fellowship and those that offer solitude. When you find them, you can subject them to a quick checklist: they may or may not be in good physical shape, like the last remaining tollhouse on the I&M, later a tiny barbershop, and now budgeted for restoration by the Illinois Department of Natural Resources. If the places you find are still relatively intact or retain some unimpaired essence, they may no longer be easy to get to; conversely, they sometimes seem hidden, even when they're right around the corner, because they've recently disappeared behind someone's fence or wall or heap of something – or, like the still sturdy floors, or footprints, of long-gone blast furnaces in Joliet, they've slowly been walled off by overgrowth.

The trickier part is that, at the same time, you're also looking inward, for interior shadows that over the course of a generation may have silently fallen across even the brightest qualities of a place – uncleared-up misunderstandings and other tensions; partly digested information and assumptions and fears that can slide through us or take up residence somewhere just beyond our awareness, so that we start to disengage from the strengths of a place, shunning it, while saying to ourselves, *It's not what it used to be.*

Some people, when talking about how places change, explain that "communities vote with their feet" – meaning that if things get bad you can always pack up and leave. Bolting and restlessness are certainly a long-standing part of our inheritance; we're by far the most mobile society that has ever existed, and the turnover never stops. Every year, one of every six Americans finds a new home – moving up, moving over, or moving far, far away, winding up, often enough, thousands of miles from what had been home. "As decades pass," in the words of a recent Worldwatch paper, "whole industries rise, fall, and move quickly across the landscape."

Of course, there are always people who have to hunker down, make do, and stay put, for financial or family reasons. But what if leaving were entirely optional, only you're not sure it's the right option? When does it make sense to stand your ground? What if you suspect that the whole vote-with-your-feet election itself has been rigged – if you know in your heart that you'd like to stay, but you frustratingly feel that every toehold that might keep you in place is unsupported by the community or is actively under siege? What if you have a knockout of an idea for making things better, but you don't know how to pull together all the people in town who might be reaching out for something very much like what you're already thinking?

FINDING A HOME FOR SPECIAL PLACES

"Lovable objects" and "areas where awe lingers" – the new move to renew America emerging within the Prairie Passage and elsewhere around the coun-

Plate 2. The tree-lined canal towpath is a refuge for wildlife, including the great blue heron, standing at the edge of the canal midway down the bank in this view, and egrets, who fish in the canal during their annual migrations along the valley's flyway.

try is slowly giving us a new nationally generated vocabulary for talking about and working with the qualities that mean the most to us in the places we admire. The new terms for these places can pop up anywhere – and then can explain every other area that is rediscovering itself. Experiences in the Northwest and the Southeast help us understand why the eye will linger on several groups of photographs in *Prairie Passage* – the large-scale landscapes, for instance, of woods, prairies, and bluffs; and the more intimate pictures of the towpath that runs beside the canal.

In Portland, Oregon, a confident and prospering community that has been re-examining itself because it's worried that it might get swamped by its own prosperity, researchers at a local university several years ago came up with the phrase "two paychecks" as a way of discussing landscapes. Talking to Portlanders, they again and again heard about all the good jobs there – and in addition kept hearing about how, when people got home from these well-paying jobs, they could walk out the front door, or at least drive out of the driveway, and within minutes be enveloped by spectacular scenery – scenery that, for Portland to keep its edge, has to stay both intact and within easy reach.

"Sacred sites," a phrase that helps explain the strong pull exerted by the I&M's unassertive towpath, is being used by communities prospecting for hidden value. But it traces back to one specific place, Manteo, North Carolina, a small offshore town near the Outer Banks. In this once prosperous community, the paychecks fifteen years ago suddenly started to disappear. Fishing, the town's traditional business, began to founder, so Manteo decided to welcome tourists. But it didn't want to be shouldered aside by the newcomers it was beckoning. To save the town's sense of itself, community-based planners engaged local citizens in conversation and drew up a list of the places that held Manteo together as a community.

The results surprised everybody, because they included some of the most unlovely and unhistoric spots in town, like the parking lot behind the Post Office and a modest diner a block away – the two places where everybody gathered every morning to get reacquainted. At the town meeting where these findings were announced, one Mantean stood up and said, "Why, these places are as sacred to us as our churches and cemeteries!" – thereby inadvertently coining a planning term.

Seventy years ago, Benton MacKaye, a forester and regional planner who is still revered along the East Coast as the father of the 2,100-mile-long Appalachian Trail between Maine and Georgia, put forward the view – it remains a notion without a nickname – that to stay healthy, all people, whatever their circumstances, need regular and ready access to at least three kinds of surroundings. Cities and towns, MacKaye said, strengthen our ties with

2. *I&M Canal and towpath, Gebhard Woods State Park, Morris.*

each other and with the world of ideas; wild places reawaken in us our sense of kinship with the rest of creation; and farmland reminds us that ten thousand years ago, at the dawn of civilization, humanity entered into a lasting partnership with the life forces of the planet. MacKaye thought that once these relationships had been secured in our lives, each of us would have a better chance to start thinking, together with other people, about the issues that affect us all, such as how to get along with each other and how to keep the planet stable enough so it can continue to sustain life.

Several economists have recently pointed out that, as the mechanics of production change and offices and factories are no longer so tied down to some particular supply source or workforce, businesses are increasingly pulled toward the places people already know they want to be in. But, like it or not, these preferred places can seldom make a go of things by themselves. As planners keep pointing out, another set of forces is also at work: the deep countryside hundreds of miles away from the big cities is emptying out, and most Americans (80 percent now, and 90 percent only a few years from now) live in enormous metropolitan areas that have enmeshed the economies of older cities with those of newer suburbs, even if neither group has given much thought to the other's needs.

We're also getting a clearer picture that the places people want to be in are good for our physical health and mental well-being. Public health evidence points, for instance, to the existence of "healing landscapes," a concept that emerged when it was discovered that patients recovering from surgery who can see trees or a park from their hospital windows, instead of blank brick walls, get better faster and go home sooner.

Already we have an informal name for places like the Prairie Passage that can point to multiple paychecks, sacred sites, and healing landscapes and that, at the same time, have a resolute band of people working to make sure that, whatever comes, the strengths of the community will remain available at least long enough so that the next generation can decide for themselves whether to re-renew the promise for their own children. Such places with such citizens are called "special places." The term is an adaptation. Beginning in the late nineteenth century, Americans who recognized the value of superb wilderness landscapes campaigned to have the naturalness of those special places protected as public parks. In the 125 years since Yellowstone was set aside as America's (and the world's) first national park, we have both fulfilled and outgrown that original dream.

What we have created is the world's most extensive system of natural sanctuaries, and from a planetary point of view we are, despite lapses, within striking distance of setting aside enough land to permit the healing of the earth's ecosystems and watersheds. But along the way, without quite defining it, we've been creating a second legacy, a parallel network of lived-in landscapes. These inhabited and semi-inhabited places take up at least as much room as the wild places that remain. And in the aggregate, they have as much deep meaning for us as the wild lands just beyond them.

The old buy-it-up-and-set-it-aside national parks solution is irrelevant to this new situation, because humanized landscapes present a separate kind of complexity. This doesn't just mean that, unlike protected wilderness parks, they're mostly made up of private property. The truly complicating factor is that, in America's new special places, much of the private property has sometimes rapidly and sometimes gradually taken on community-sustaining functions that don't appear on title deeds – with the result that it now benefits entire communities as much as it does the owners of the moment. The "takings" clause of the U.S. Constitution properly guarantees that no private property may be expropriated for public purposes unless the owners receive full value for what they're giving up. But because the situation hadn't yet presented itself in the eighteenth century, the Constitution doesn't incorporate a "givings" clause that sets up a mechanism for identifying, working with, and further enhancing the unvoiced public value that private property often begins to accumulate in special places.

PUBLIC RIGHTS

The idea that "public rights" can adhere to privately owned land, as Charles E. Little, America's leading environmental writer on public landscapes, has pointed out, was first voiced by one of humanity's greatest poets; it appeared in print in 1810, in a short guidebook to the English Lake District written by William Wordsworth. The consummate beauty of that area, Wordsworth wrote, the totality created and sustained by its hills, ponds, villages, farms, and woods, spoke so feelingly to every succeeding generation of the English people that it had come to constitute "a sort of national property, in which every man has a right and interest who has an eye to see and a heart to enjoy."

Fifty years ago, just after World War II, the English set up their own national park system as a way of celebrating the peace, and they modeled it on the Wordsworthian, or "green-line," approach. This means calling a park into being by taking a map and drawing a green line around the outermost limits of a special place. It's an act both imaginary and real – imaginary, because as far as ownership is concerned it's exactly as it was, both inside the line and out; and real, because now the place has public standing.

In the special place now officially treasured as the Lake District National Park, for instance, national and local government agencies own almost no land at all. A quarter of the land is in the hands

Figure 5. This bike rental shop in Utica, near Starved Rock State Park, promotes the I&M Canal State Trail, which is open to hikers, cyclists, joggers, cross-country skiers, and snowmobilers. Funding is in place to continue the trail to the Chicago Portage site at the edge of Chicago, creating a continuous trail system that would form an unbroken recreational link between Chicago's western edge and quiet rural towns such as Utica.

of a much-admired, scholarly, nonprofit group of museum and parks administrators called the National Trust; the other three-quarters is privately held. The government, whose role has been strictly limited by careful design, protects the national interest in the Lake District by championing its continuity, so that changes, when they come (as of course they must), can be absorbed without compromising any of the recreational, historic, ecological, and scenic qualities that have already rewarded so many eyes and hearts.

Campaigning to bring the qualities of a special place into sharper focus is usually quiet, underfunded work. The one ground rule is that nobody can force anybody to do anything – which makes it sound like it works by consensus, but that's a grudging word, often only a synonym for a truce, whereas this process can really be said to exist only whenever or wherever or for as long as people are acting in harmony. Despite all this, it may pop up almost anywhere and can be contagious, even on first glance. Picking up this book, for instance, and leafing through it is a contact point, an invitation to get involved, to take up the burden, to have some fun. It's hard not to start contrasting the photographs on these pages with pictures of best-loved places that every mind accumulates and holds onto dearly. Getting personal about places can lead straight into becoming a participant.

THE TECHNOLOGY OF OPTIMISM

There is, however, a caution: the search for specialness in places does imply altering the way the winds of change sweep through people's minds. This is an intricate subject in any society, and in ours we start with one strike against us, since we have a default setting to skeptical. Some of our so-deeply-ingrained-as-to-seem-almost-instinctive responses to places or people have been reinforced and underscored by the wise proverbs and folk tales handed down to us from earlier cultures that use unforgettable images to steer us away from false hopes and delusions.

Americans have a sure sense that if someone's foolish enough to try to make a silk purse out of a sow's ear, we're going to know about it; and we don't doubt that if some emperor actually passes us on the street, we'll be able to tell if he's got any clothes on. But we may have trouble finding our way to hope because our "technology of optimism" has rusty parts and missing pieces; and maybe, in consequence, we are too ready to assume that hope is hard to come by.

What might you do, for instance, if you had a valuable silk purse that any number of your friends and neighbors could also use, and you found out that you couldn't even give it away because they were convinced, some of them almost bitterly so, that you were trying to hand them a sow's ear? What would you say to help them see a nearby monarch, gorgeously robed if somewhat travel stained, whom they've shunned because they think they've already been given authoritative information about his utter nakedness?

GETTING DOWN TO CASES: THE CHICAGO OUTLET VALLEY

These are not hypothetical questions but in fact very practical ones: they summarize the dangerous, frustrating circumstances that residents of a real and special place, the Chicago Outlet Valley, found themselves facing almost two decades ago. Not that anyone at the outset was seeing the situation in quite these terms. The valley, narrow as it is,

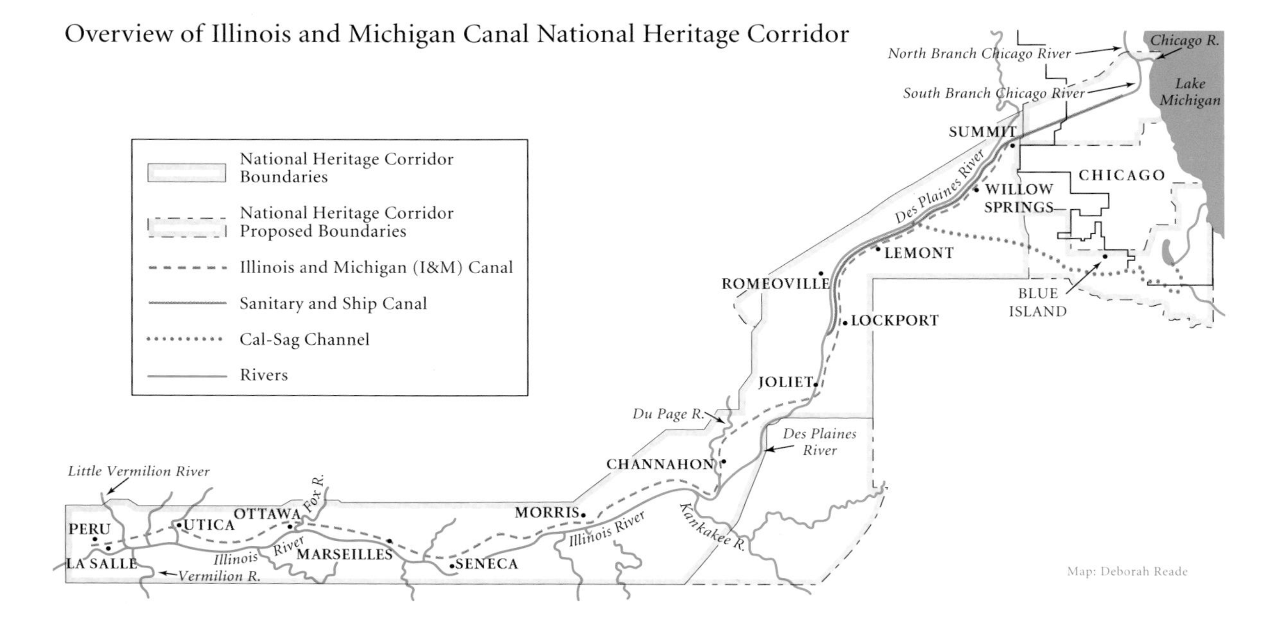

Overview of Illinois and Michigan Canal National Heritage Corridor

embraces almost three hundred thousand acres along its hundred-mile length and is home and workplace for more than a million people. On a map and from the air it has a kind of quarter-to-two shape: oversimplifying only slightly, it's the land around two liquid straight lines, part river and part canal, that meet at an angle. The hour hand, about forty-five miles long, stretches directly southwest from Lake Michigan at the Navy Pier in the very center of Chicago, edges the Loop, slices through the Southwest Side, and cuts past the old industrial city of Joliet to a small village called Channahon. The minute hand runs west for about fifty miles from Channahon to the twin mid-state Illinois river towns of Peru and La Salle. To be more precise, it's a three-pronged, 1:45:12 landscape; the system's second hand, the Cal-Sag, another canal-and-river combination, leaves the lake at the Port of Chicago at the city's Indiana border, the far southeast corner, runs through the town of Blue Island, and flows into the hour hand about halfway between Joliet and Chicago.

In the 1830s, when construction began on the I&M Canal, the Chicago Outlet Valley suddenly became a hugely important part of inventing modern America. Facing crisis in the late 1970s and early 1980s, the valley took on a new role in history; this was the moment "Rustbelt" became a word on the nightly news. Industrial jobs that had seemed permanent and inheritable vanished, never to reappear. Factories, steel mills, and refineries closed, and overnight hundreds of people lost lifelong jobs. In Joliet, the largest valley settlement outside Chicago, 26 percent of the population was out of work, the highest unemployment rate in the country.

With jobs drying up, the issue valley residents had to face seemed exacting, austere, clear-cut: Was there any kind of future to look forward to? Soon it became apparent that this hardheaded, practical debate was really about the present, and about how to put body and soul together, and about which part of the spectrum of perceptions between optimism and pessimism could be trusted. You weren't

likely to think the area had much promise unless you felt that past promises had been kept, and that the valley, despite the disappearance of so many jobs, was still special, still a place that made life worthwhile. The future, therefore, would begin with how people read the valley's story-so-far and whether their ties to their surroundings had enough resilience to lead them forward.

There were no ready answers. The Chicago Outlet Valley's specialness had long ago become so elusive for so many people that for most of a century it had been almost hidden in plain sight – uncelebrated by some of its own and ignored by many neighbors for whom it was no longer a real place. It was Rip Van Winkle played backward – as if the valley had stayed awake to itself, for the most part,

Figure 6. Lemont, now one of the fastest-growing areas in metropolitan Chicago, evolved as a community of quarry and canal workers. The church steeples nestled in the bluffs reflect the village's settlement by Polish, Irish, Ukrainian, and Slavic immigrants. Newcomers are working with long-time residents to protect Lemont's special qualities. Handsome local dolomite façades have been preserved, and new businesses serve residents and attract visitors.

Figure 7. The Grundy County Courthouse square in Morris is home to several monuments, including this cedar pole that once marked the burial mound of the Potawatomi chief Nuquette. Nineteen burial mounds dating from the Upper Mississippian period (A.D. 1200–1500) lined the river in Morris when the canal was constructed. In 1925 the Daughters of the American Revolution installed the ceremonial pole in the courthouse square.

while everyone else nearby had fallen asleep. Twenty years ago, most Americans had never visited the valley; or, if they had zoomed past it on the then-new interstate that skirts its northern edge, they weren't aware later on that that was what they had done.

Although the valley had its admirers around Illinois, it couldn't look to its nearby neighbors for help, because so many Chicago residents had long ago stopped looking southwest; or, to complicate matters further, they looked only at the farthest-away and southernmost end of the valley, a hundred miles distant, which since 1911 had been set aside as a beloved and always-returned-to cliffside state park, Starved Rock. Oddly enough, it's possible to give a precise date to the moment when Chicagoans began their withdrawal of affection for the valley: 1882, when Mrs. Potter Palmer, wife of the developer of the Palmer House and leader of Chicago society whose collection of Impressionists forms the nucleus of the Art Institute's holdings, abandoned her elegant South Side mansion in what had been until then the most fashionable part of town and built an enormous new mansion on the North Side's empty lands, along Lake Shore Drive.

It was an act that set in motion a splintering of Chicago, once a south- and southwest-facing town and now a city with no fixed gaze – so that South and Southwest Siders looked inward, to themselves, or, for restoration, turned east to the lake or southeast to the nearby Indiana dunes; while North Siders, when they thought of open lands, began looking so far north that their eyes came to rest on Wisconsin lakes fifty miles distant. For almost four generations, the far view to the southwest was obscured. The Outlet Valley and its many towns and cities disappeared from Chicago's sight – or were seen, distantly and inaccurately, as places of problems, not strengths.

The South Side's sewage and steel mills, though belonging to the city itself, and not the people living farther downstream, obscured the valley from many Chicagoans' view. Later generations were again deflected away from sympathy for the valley by South Side events – parts of it became vice districts: the "Levee," the "Cheyenne," and the "Tenderloin." Al Capone made his headquarters there at the Lexington Hotel. Later, and more tragically, there were race riots, as the so-called Great Migration and other waves of African-American resettlement poured people into the South Side ghetto once known as the "Black Belt" – it grew from fifteen thousand people in 1890 to a quarter of a million forty years later.

PUTTING THE GREAT SPAN AND OTHER TIME LINES TO WORK

Compounding the valley's troubles, the problems of the early 1980s showed that valley residents had not yet forged a unified view of themselves. In

Ceremonial Time, a 1984 book about the full post-glacial history of a now sprawl-nibbled town in eastern Massachusetts, John Hanson Mitchell writes that he first learned to see continuity in the midst of change when a Native American whose people had long ago moved away from the state told him that, in their own minds, they had maintained their residence. That was because the land still had the same contours and so would be recognizable to descendants of the Native Americans who had known it. Mitchell called this unbroken reality "ceremonial time."

In the Outlet Valley, modern settlement reaches back five or six generations; almost five hundred generations of Native Americans preceded them, but in the early 1830s, in fulfillment of a national development policy officially known as "Indian Removal," they had departed to land west of the Mississippi River. Recent research suggests that in northern Illinois ceremonial time has some physical basis – that many first Americans in fact stayed behind and eventually, without talking about it, intermarried with those who came after them, so that at least some contemporary bloodlines in the area reach back to the glaciers.

In the meantime, the newcomers set up their own time lines and by the 1980s had been in place long enough to feel the resonance of what is sometimes called the "Great Span" – a way of defining memory's reach within a community. Firsthand

memories of a place, the most compelling we have, are a kind of extension ladder for long-settled families. Today's adults still find real what their grandparents told them long ago. And if a family has stayed put for more than a century, then what these adults have heard includes stories about the place that their grandparents picked up as small children from their own grandparents.

Those earliest Great Span memories that can still be carried forward extend back, in the Chicago Outlet Valley, to frontier days and pre-industrial times. Just as John Hanson Mitchell didn't need to have been born a Native American to begin to feel the pull of ceremonial time, you don't have to come from a five-generation valley family to tap into the knowledge preserved by the Great Span – it's in the air. Some valley people today can, for instance, look at a large, late nineteenth-century white frame farmhouse and see the small log cabin that still exists at the heart of the much later building that now cloaks it. They're in touch with and esteem much about the Chicago Outlet Valley that didn't disappear when its factory jobs started vanishing.

By contrast, for some valley residents, people who had previously seemed just as deep-rooted, jobs had been the anchor, not the valley itself; all their lives they had known only one compelling reason for wanting to stay put. But it was curious that you couldn't have told in advance who was attuned to what – some oldtimers were ready to leave; many newcomers were eager to stick around. Rallying around strengths that still called out was the survival strategy that valley people who could hear them eventually evolved to stave off despair and depopulation.

One resident spoke of disillusionment: "I was just always so depressed. A beautiful, old empty schoolhouse in the middle of town, built of the native yellow valley limestone, was about to be torn down simply because nobody had thought of anything else to do with it. A lush, flat, and very rare patch of wet prairie down by the river" – a remnant of the valley's presettlement landscapes and home to the world's largest population of leafy prairie clover, which grows globally in only three locations – "was about to be buried under muck dredged from a nearby canal by engineers who could see how empty it was but missed seeing how full it was – of life and of meaning. So we took our stand and saved these places."

THE HERITAGE CORRIDOR

The Chicago Outlet Valley was the first sliver of America to take on the risk of re-evaluating itself on this scale. It also became the first American special place to be nationally recognized for attacking problems by burnishing specialness: under unprecedented legislation passed in 1984 by a Democratic Congress and signed into law by a

Republican president, the entire valley became the country's first National Heritage Corridor. With this official federal designation, the valley became a uniquely American green-line park. Valley land, as in English green-line parks, remains, and will never cease to be, predominantly privately owned. The American law acknowledges, as English laws do, that because the Outlet Valley is a special place, public rights have become attached to its private property.

But in the National Heritage Corridor the federal government has not taken on the mission of maintaining the cohesiveness of these public rights; it instead set up an arena in which volunteers – citizens, businesses, nonprofit groups, foundations, and even agencies within local and state govern-

Figure 8. The acres of wetland preserved along Romeoville's Centennial Trail in the Des Plaines River valley provide habitat for wildlife and protect native Illinois plants such as the yellow flag iris. Forest preserve districts of three different counties formed a partnership with the Metropolitan Water Reclamation District to create this trail.

Plate 3. Midewin, which means "healing society" in the Potawatomi language, is the name of the new National Tallgrass Prairie being created on 19,000 acres of the former Joliet Army Arsenal, once the site of the world's largest TNT factory. The factory was surrounded by pastures and significant natural resources – including prairie groves, dolomite prairies, upland forests, streams, wetlands, and seeps – that provide habitats for hundreds of species of birds, native plants, animals, and fish. The wetland shown here will serve as a buffer between the prairie park and an industrial park, which will be built after the remains of the factory, shown in the distance, are removed.

ments – are encouraged to step forward to champion the public interest. Within the corridor the federal government speaks softly and has set aside its big stick; the only federal agency in residence is a small office of the National Park Service, whose only authority is to advise, urge, and facilitate the reaching of agreements.

And agreements are being reached. Among the most significant are those that broaden public rights within already publicly owned pieces of land. For example, there is now a trails coalition of nonprofit park advocates, county park agencies, a regional water district, and the state transportation department; it's brought in tens of millions of dollars of federal highway money to thread the valley together by means of a continuous trail, extending the 61.5-mile-long I&M Canal State Trail along the canal's 150-year-old towpath. The Canal Trail now runs through the western end of the valley, but it will be stretched far enough to reach the city limits of Chicago. The twenty new trail miles – they're called the Centennial Trail – run through wild land that has long belonged to the Metropolitan Water Reclamation District.

A separately arrived-at consensus among business interests, conservationists, government leaders, and park advocates has converted a vast and surplus army arsenal outside Joliet into Midewin, more than nineteen thousand acres of new public parkland that will be restored as tallgrass prairie and once again grazed by bison and elk. Midewin will be the largest tallgrass prairie east of the Mississippi. Several thousand additional acres of former arsenal property will be put to other uses, such as a national veterans cemetery and an industrial park to create new jobs for the Joliet area.

With the coming of Midewin, the Chicago Outlet Valley will now be both anchored and connected by public rights – Starved Rock, Midewin, and the Palos Forest Preserve are outstanding protected wildlands at the far end of the valley, in the middle, and up near the city end. And they'll be yoked together by the Canal Trail and the Centennial Trail. Time lines have joined forces – it's a new fusion of landscapes that live in ceremonial time and paths that were first thought of back at the beginning of the Great Span. Nonprofit groups are particularly important to the success of these imaginative and large-scale corridor projects – as this book, conceived and commissioned by the Canal Corridor Association, so clearly demonstrates.

Enthusiasts sometimes call the region a "partnership park," a term that suggests cooperation, something that is both binding and fragile. Whenever partnerships emerge, the valley becomes more parklike. But that endures only as long as the partnerships do. This is a story, in other words, with a happy middle, because after almost fifteen years the founders have gotten the vision out of

3. *Joliet Army Arsenal/Midewin National Tallgrass Prairie.*

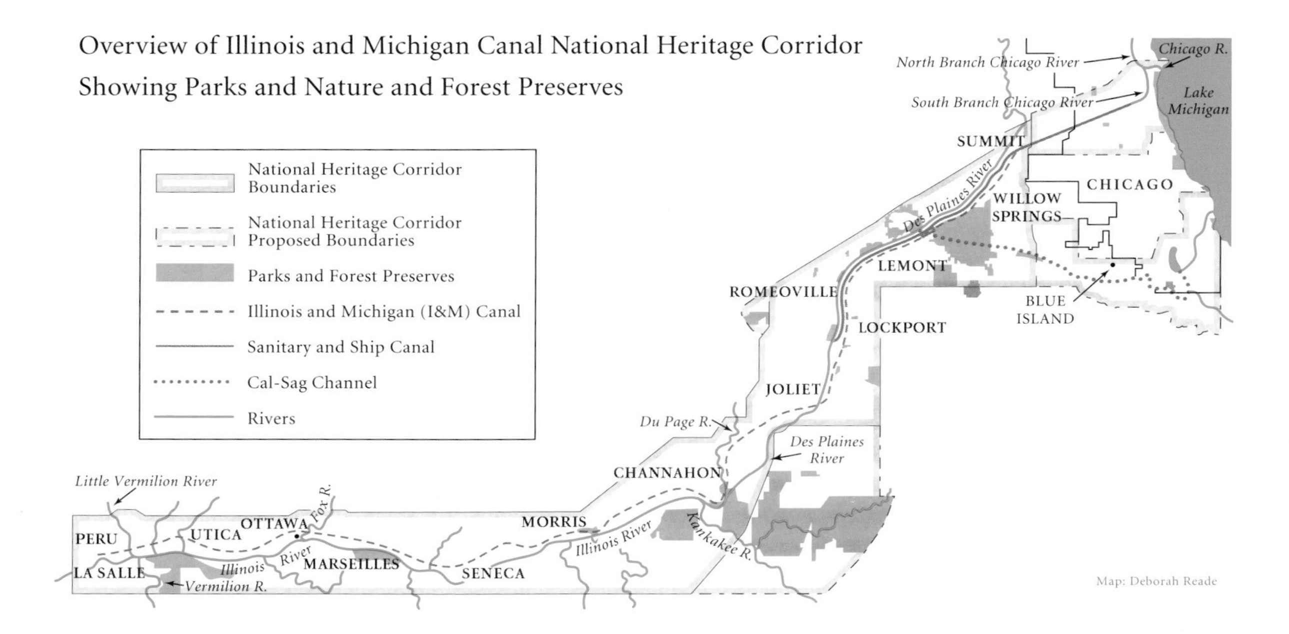

Overview of Illinois and Michigan Canal National Heritage Corridor Showing Parks and Nature and Forest Preserves

their own heads and into those of many other people. It might take another fifteen years before anyone can announce a happy ending or hope to show that the effects of this vision have permeated the lives of everyone in the valley.

The next parts of the story will take new directions:

* The valley's population has stabilized; indeed, it's headed upward, and a new question is how the growth associated with malls and sprawl will respond to a vision of the valley that's still being refreshed. Newcomers are arriving to be close to the jobs being created west of Chicago. Will they respond positively to what's already been created by the valley's renewers?

* Without knowing the outcome, the rest of the country is already asking to join in. The United States now has fourteen additional congressionally designated national heritage areas and corridors. And there are fifty or sixty other candidate areas eager for admission. People are looking to the Chicago Outlet Valley for answers. Can it find them even while it's still questioning itself?

TWO CANALS CHANGE HISTORY

More than 160 years ago, a small and brand-new group of midwesterners became, in effect, the fifth glacier to sweep across northern Illinois, vastly, lastingly, and purposefully affecting both the local landscape and people halfway across the country. They were the canal builders. It was a project that, as enunciated by President James Madison, had become a national strategic goal, and it was a new state's dearest dream. The Illinois state line had already been moved forty miles north to keep even the smallest part of the new canal from being built on Wisconsin soil.

But the idea had been inspired by a quick insight into the underlying water structure of the place, and how it could be rearranged, that had struck the valley's first European visitors – two young Frenchmen, a twenty-seven-year-old explorer,

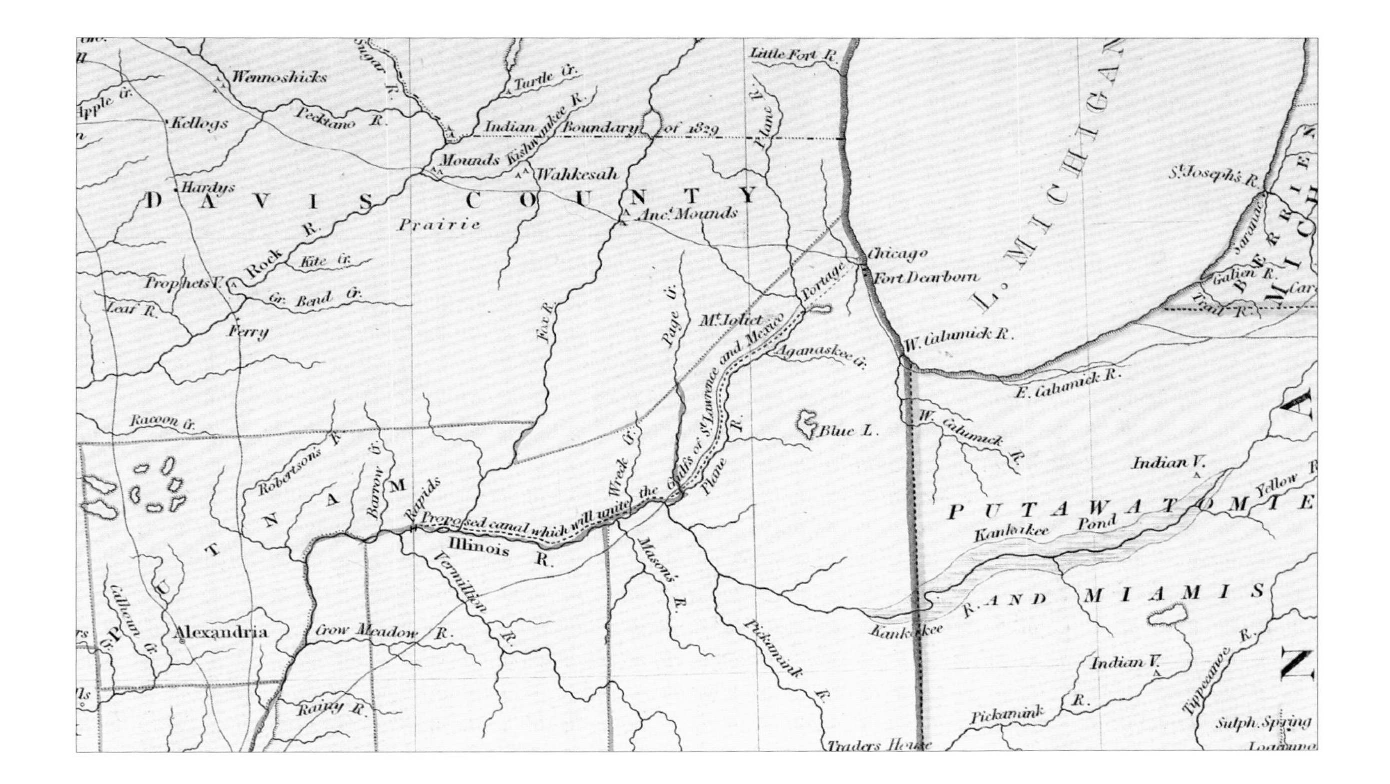

Louis Jolliet, and Jacques Marquette, a priest in his mid-thirties, who came through in 1673 only because Native American guides were showing them a shortcut home to Canada. Jolliet, a would-be empire builder, pulling his canoe across a low hill near Lake Michigan, had immediately understood that he was crossing a continental divide as commanding as the snow-capped Rockies: the unremarkable hill is part of a dividing line between the waters of the East Coast and the waters of the Midwest. Raindrops that fall on one side of the hill flow through the Great Lakes and down Niagara Falls into the Atlantic Ocean; rain hitting the other side rolls down the Mississippi River into the Gulf of Mexico.

The valley's nineteenth-century newcomers, using only picks and shovels, hand-dug a slender, shallow, nintey-seven-mile-long canal, the Illinois and Michigan, and cutting through the small hill brought lake waters into proximity with those of the Illinois River for the first time since the earlier glaciers had receded. By 1848, when mule-drawn

Figure 9. Detail of a map entitled "North America: Sheet IX, Parts of Missouri, Illinois and Indiana," 1833. (Courtesy of the MacLean Collection.)

barges started moving up and down the I&M, two of the country's three greatest watersheds had been connected, and in that moment, what the East Coast produced and what the Midwest grew could finally be exchanged with ease. Chicago, though tabletop flat, sat astride the divide and was the place where the deals could be made.

This one heroic excavation project, which was largely the work of Irish immigrants living in primitive and badly provisioned tent camps (cholera alone claimed hundreds of lives), transformed the Chicago Outlet Valley into a modern place of agriculture and industry. At the same time, the canal gave Chicago, the "Golden Funnel," as some called the new terminus town at the north end of the canal, such a powerful, prerailroad boost that by 1893, the year of the Columbian Exposition, Chicago was the first settlement in the history of the world to grow from virtual emptiness into a city of a million people in little more than half a century.

Chicago may be the I&M Canal's most visible accomplishment, but less obviously – if just as enduringly – the canal brought with it a national shifting of allegiances and strengths that in the pre–Civil War years buttressed the North and diminished the South. Precanal trade that had once gone to St. Louis and New Orleans was so thoroughly diverted to Chicago that the Mississippi River, or at least the trade it carried, now poured north. Settlement patterns also changed. After the canal came, the Old Northwest, as the northern Midwest had once been known, in the days when the Mississippi was the country's western border, began to fill up differently. Previously Illinois had been getting much of its new population from the South; after the canal opened, most new settlers were antislavery northeasterners or Europeans who were themselves refugees from repression.

Having created Chicago in the second quarter of the nineteenth century with a canal, the waterways of the valley toward the end of the century had to rescue the city, retrofitting it with a second canal, the Sanitary and Ship Canal, four and a half times as deep and almost three times as wide as the first. This new canal kept Chicago from becoming the first city in history to be deserted by a million people nearly overnight. If it was altogether unexpected that Jolliet and Marquette, those early European visitors to the valley, could in 1673 have seen almost at a glance the continent-altering potential of slicing through a single hill, the late nineteenth-century engineers who built the Sanitary Canal imagined an even more staggering act of water manipulation.

The first canal made Chicago the logical location for a great city, but the lakeside marshes were otherwise ill suited for human habitation, because water that people made dirty couldn't drain away. Instead, this water poured into the lake itself,

Plate 4. The Chicago River is now lined by a canyon of office buildings, bearing little resemblance to the busy water highway that stimulated the city's meteoric growth from a hamlet of a hundred people in 1830, to a town of twenty thousand in 1848, to a regional population today of eight million.

4. *South Branch of the Chicago River, looking north to the Jackson Boulevard Bridge from the Van Buren Street Bridge.*

Figure 10. The noted Civil War photographer George Barnard captured this image of the postfire destruction along the Chicago River, looking northeast from Lake Street and South Water Street (later West Wacker Drive). The Great Fire of 1871 destroyed some seventeen thousand buildings in a "burnt district" that was over four miles long and three-quarters of a mile wide. Convection whirls created tornadoes of fire that sent burning lumber and debris across the Chicago River. Many residents took refuge in the lake while the flames destroyed their city, while others fled to the open prairie to the northwest. Chicago gained national attention because of the disaster and because it immediately began rebuilding, "like a Phoenix rising from the ashes." (Courtesy of the Chicago Architectural Photographing Co., David R. Phillips.)

which the city needed for drinking water. The real devastation that befell Chicago in 1871 was not the Great Fire, which consumed thousands of buildings but only took the lives of three hundred people, but a cholera epidemic that killed tens of thousands of people. The solution of the sanitary engineers was to turn the water flow around. The I&M Canal commissioners tried at first to deepen the I&M – halfheartedly and unsuccessfully. The sanitary engineers then dug a second, parallel canal – and the new canal was so wide and so deep that lake water, which since glacial times had flowed east toward Niagara Falls and the St. Lawrence River, reversed course and poured southwest down the Illinois River.

There were real fears that the Sanitary Canal project – its enormity required gigantic and specially devised excavation machines later duplicated in Central America for the digging of the Panama Canal – would work too well and that, as a result, Niagara would run dry. The fears were groundless, as it turned out, and the project, which changed

Figure 11. The massive Chicago Drainage Canal (later the Sanitary and Ship Canal) was completed in 1900 and extended twenty-eight miles from Chicago to Lockport. It successfully reversed the flow of the Chicago River, causing the city's sewage to flow southwest and away from Lake Michigan, which was the city's source of drinking water. (1895 photograph courtesy of the Metropolitan Water Reclamation District.)

the face of the city by bringing in thousands of black and Polish workers, also triumphantly achieved its original purpose and cleansed the city and kept the lake water clear.

MUCH SIMPLE BEING THERE

These are stories that enrich the Upper Illinois River Valley and pervade every picture in this book. The magisterial sweep of Edward Ranney's landscape photographs provide the first comprehensive depiction, at once authoritative, unflinching, and deeply appreciative, as is his style, of current conditions in the valley. Only a photographer as accomplished as Ranney – someone who can keep a subject unswervingly in focus – could do justice to a landscape so complicated, so contradictory, and so thoroughly alive. He ringingly demonstrates that landscape photography can be a powerful new weapon in the arsenal of optimism, because his photographer's eye is quicker than the uninformed doubt or fear that would reject a place unseen.

Fifteen years from now, when the Illinois and Michigan Canal National Heritage Corridor is reaching its thirtieth birthday, Edward Ranney's consummate and panoramic portraits will again occupy a place of honor at the celebrations. People will marvel at the fact that, way back in 1998, when the canal had not yet been universally rediscovered, he saw the full sweep of this hundred-mile-long landscape and looked past all its complications to the strong, simple forces that organize the place – the canal and the valley that holds it.

Great landscape photographers are shortcut takers, place rescuers, world changers, truth tellers, alchemists, people who cram a hidden, extra, soul-feeding layer into every picture. As they roam the earth, some of them seem to have left geography behind, acquiring instead the range of astronomers who photograph patterns created at endless distances and long-ago ages. Ranney is one of these global explorers, exposing images at the far ends of the earth that stretch our understanding by fixing in our minds the reality and value of places and people we'll never see ourselves. In his roamings since the 1960s, he has repeatedly returned to Peru's most challenging landscapes, to photograph remote Inca ruins in the high Andes and pre-Columbian sites in oceanfront deserts that even the hardiest travelers might bypass.

But it is not where they go that determines what the greatest photographers are capable of seeing. Because when they work at home they can show us the living spirit of the nearby, treasures in the everyday world that might always have been ours but that we've made ourselves inaccessible to. In the early 1970s, the great American landscape and portrait photographer Paul Strand, who was then already eighty-three, was asked how it was that, wherever he went, he could take a picture that recorded not just a single moment in time but the whole life of a person up to and including that moment; or the entire history of a town since its founding; or even the growth and decay of a mountain. He said that there was no trick to any of it, that these were merely the kinds of things you started to notice about places and people after "much looking, much simple being there."

"It is the special capability of photography," Edward Ranney has written in the preface to his 1982 book, *Monuments of the Incas*, "to reveal meanings not apparent before." For Ranney, the "much looking" part of his business is an active, rugged, and very three-dimensional undertaking. As you can see just by glancing through *Prairie Passage*, Ranney's eye has been everywhere in and above the Canal Corridor. He works, as America's first landscape photographers did, with a view camera – the kind that sits imposingly on a tripod – although his is a slightly smaller, more modern version that flips back on a hinge, allowing him to walk hands free and haul the camera around on his shoulder. Ranney gets deep inside landscapes – in the valley he's waded through swamps, peered inside machinery, and scrambled up tall bridge towers. He's even chartered small planes, for pictures with a more maplike perspective; but for these shots he makes use of a conventional, small hand camera.

Ranney's mind's eye is at rest – wide-open, appreciative, deeply drinking in his surroundings. There's a powerful stillness at the core of his work, a "much simple being there" that carries forward Strand's approach to picture taking and over a twenty-five-year-span has produced a new generation of similarly profound, revealing, and resonant images. He is drawn to special places – not just the mountains and deserts of Peru but the high plains of New Mexico (where he has lived since 1970), Wordsworth's Lake District, and the Central American lowlands where the Maya built their temples. Ranney takes pictures of time lines; the todays in his pictures are open-ended, stretching back for centuries or more – so that looking at one of his photographs is almost like putting on a pair of four-dimensional glasses.

CHIEF SHABBONA

Edward Ranney's Canal Corridor pictures continue in his bold archival tradition of rescuing-by-recording-truthfully some of the special places of the world, whether currently adored or underappreciated. Once again, he vividly demonstrates the still-hereness of the long gone. These picture are brimming with what's real because they've been emptied of preconceptions. What emerges is the arc of time, the living spirit of the once-upon-a-time.

Deep in this book is a photograph of a mid-nineteenth-century portrait in a gilt frame that the eye seems drawn to even before the mind is quite ready to say why. It's typical of the quiet friendliness with which Ranney photographs special landscapes that he can set before us an image that clearly fascinates him without suggesting that he thinks we ought to pay special attention to it. The painting, which shows a massively built, middle-aged Native American chief, sitting as calmly and as implacably as a boulder, hangs in the window of fire department headquarters in Morris, Illinois, a town of about fifteen thousand people with a strong sense of what it has accomplished over the years.

Morris has a handsome, four-generations-old, late-Victorian downtown that it's proud of, anchored by a department store still owned by a local family and a county courthouse that's been in business for more than a century and a half; it sits amid superb farmland in the heart of the Upper Illinois River Valley. The first thing you notice in Ranney's photograph of the chief is not the chief himself but something far more resplendent –

a nineteenth-century fire truck standing in front of the portrait, a cherished artifact that has recently been so lovingly cared for that it's almost aglow with paint and polish. In the forcefulness of its newly reacquired sparkle, this modest horse-drawn pumper not much larger than a cart, with a buggy's mammoth, clattering wooden wheels, seems poised, as you contemplate it with Ranney, to take on some urgently required task that will do more than merely convey the message of never-faltering protection and watchfulness that the Morris Fire Department is openly broadcasting to the town by putting it on display.

Here, you start to think, is a machine so charged with present affection and past purpose, so fussed over, mended, and tended, that it ought somehow to be able to return the favor and take on repair jobs back through time; surely it could sally forth, if only we knew how to activate it, and mend some pieces of the past, straighten some wrong turns – saving one house, maybe even half a dozen, from the Great Chicago Fire of October 1871 that burned for twenty-seven hours and destroyed two thousand acres of buildings.

And then Ranney shows you that the little fire-engine-that-could, this very crisp object, is already somewhat hazy and indistinct. You're looking at it through an enormous, corner plate-glass window, so gleamingly clean, like the old fire truck, that it is part mirror and carries on its surface a reflection the sidewalk and street and tall trees that would be behind you if you were standing in front of the window. At the same time, while some things are bouncing back at you from near at hand, you're also looking beyond the fire truck straight through to a street around the corner from you, because the corner office of the Morris Fire Department has two plate-glass display windows at right angles to each other.

You realize then that this is a scene that conceals as well as reveals: it gives you eyes in the back of your head, or at any rate shows you things that in other circumstances would be invisible; but it also obscures things you always expect to see unclouded. How odd – you can now see beyond the obvious, but you can't quite make out what is normally inescapable. It's at this point that you start paying closer attention to the portrait – first because it's at the meeting point of lines that by rights shouldn't be crossing (lines in the reflection and lines in the view beyond the reflection). And second, because the large eyes in the portrait are on you, with a gaze as disconcertingly direct as Washington's on the one-dollar bill. The man in the portrait – his name was Chief Shabbona, which he himself pronounced "Shab-ney" – was buried, under a boulder, in Evergreen Cemetery outside Morris almost 140 years ago. His picture, a modern charcoal and pastel drawing over an enlargement of an old photograph, is conventionally painted except for the eyes. It shows a man with a strong, square face, thick black hair curling at the sides and just going white at the temples, arching black eyebrows, a prominent nose, and a downturned mouth. He is wearing an elegantly nonchalant mixture of clothes – buckskin jacket, striped silk shirt, black cravat.

Shabbona is remembered locally as the "good Indian," or the "nice Indian," the "white man's friend." This means that, although as a younger man he fought with the British in the War of 1812, in his middle years, the age in the portrait, he saw the futility of further resistance and warned white settlers of impending attacks by Black Hawk, who in 1832 led the final, doomed war for Native American land rights in Illinois. The fire truck in Ranney's picture was named for Shabbona. Today, a prominent Morris citizen, a former County Board member, appears at local events dressed as Shabbona. But you don't have to know anything about Shabbona, or know that his defection still angers many Native Americans, to be held by the searching look in his eyes.

There is no way we can pretend to distance ourselves from that look. Shabbona, an Ottawa born in Ohio who married the daughter of a Potawatomi chief, lived most of his life in the Prairie Passage. So his are the eyes of a man who knew that valley in the eighteenth and early nineteenth centuries when it remained what it had been, most immediately, for the preceding three thousand years – a dynamic, young, postglacial wilderness. A succession of Native Americans had seen every one of those years and had close knowledge of its landmarks: open groves and deep woods sheltering packs of wolves; unending tallgrass prairies tended by giant herds of bison and elk.

Figure 12. An enlarged reproduction of this rare 1857 ambrotype of Chief Shabbona was the basis for the painting in the window of the fire station in Morris (see pl. 67). (Courtesy of the Chicago Historical Society.)

The valley of that long-ago yesterday had been a place permeated by water, with seeps, swamps, and sloughs at almost every turn, and threaded by at least a dozen prairie rivers, meandering and slow-moving but restless, with no fixed abode. Some of the rivers changed their shape twice a year, flood-

5. *Beaver dam at the Chicago Portage National Historic Site.*

in the spring, almost disappearing in the summer. And within a single lifetime they might also change their course altogether; as recently as 1805, for instance, the Calumet River, which now leaves Lake Michigan through the southeastern corner of Chicago, shifted from a route that wandered through northwestern Indiana.

What's most unexpected about Shabbona's gaze is not the composure that experiencing such sights has made possible but the promptings and questionings intimated by encountering his eyes. Like the street images caught by the plate-glass window just in front of his picture, Shabbona seems to intercept a viewer's outward looking and turn it inward, inviting us to examine afresh our own viewpoint. "Before I tell you what I have found," he seems to be saying, "tell me what you see, and hope to see, in the life around you." And there's pain in the face, too, unmasked by the composure – the same pain, you realize, that flowed through valley people. Today's valley residents are luckier, because they've been given a chance to rebuild, and that's an act that, as it sets to right the damage to places, also heals hurts within people.

Seeing Shabbona's ancient pain, and remembering the Chicago Outlet Valley's more recent pain, you may think, *How many times must we damage the things we need before we start taking proper care of them?* As Shabbona seems to be asking, *Isn't twice enough?*

Plate 5. This beaver dam marks the place where Native Americans, as well as explorers and fur traders, crossed the Chicago Portage. Located today in the midst of industry near the intersection of Harlem Avenue and the Stevenson Expressway, the beaver dam lies in a backwater of the channelized Des Plaines River. The Chicago Portage National Historic Site is protected by the Forest Preserve of Cook County as a tiny remnant of the vast marshy wetland that separated the Des Plaines and Chicago Rivers at the time of Louis Jolliet and Jacques Marquette (see pls. 8 and 22–23).

6. *Goose Lake Prairie State Park.*

INTRODUCTION

A Meeting of the Waters

EMILY J. HARRIS

Prairies filled with flowers and tall grasses, oak groves nestled along marshy rivers and creeks, and wetlands teeming with wildlife – these natural features defined northern Illinois's presettlement landscape. For thousands of years Native Americans traversed the land, establishing trading highways along the rivers and trails between the Gulf of Mexico and the Great Lakes. French explorers, in search of trade routes across the continent, were delighted to learn of the natural water passage that connected Lake Michigan to the Mississippi River through the Illinois prairies. In 1673 the explorer Louis Jolliet, upon returning from the Chicago Portage between the Chicago and Des Plaines Rivers, told his Jesuit sponsor, Father Dablon, that he had found "a very great and important advantage which will hardly be believed. . . . [W]e could go with ease to Florida [the Spanish territory that included the Gulf of Mexico] in a bark and by very easy navigation. It would be necessary to make a canal, by cutting through but half a league of prairie, to pass from the foot of Lake Michigan to the Des Plaines."

Figure 13. At the end of 1674, Fr. Jacques Marquette returned to Illionis to establish a mission near the present-day Starved Rock State Park. Delayed by illness and bad weather, he and his two assistants spent the winter in a hut they built four miles inland from Lake Michigan on the South Branch of the Chicago River near where Damen Avenue crosses the Sanitary and Ship Canal. Although Chicago was largely uninhabited at that time, Marquette encountered two French traders and a party of Illinois Indians. (From a photograph of a painting. Courtesy of the Chicago Historical Society, ICHi 26983.)

While Jolliet dreamed of a canal – and the trading empire it could build – Jacques Marquette, the priest who accompanied him on his river explorations in 1673, dedicated himself to bringing

Plate 6. Early travelers described prairies extending as far as the eye could see, echoing the Great Lakes' expanse of water with a sea of tall grasses. In 1837 Harriet Martineau wrote in *Society in America* of the prairie outside Chicago: "When I saw a settler's child tripping out of home-bounds, I had a feeling that it would never get back again. It looked like putting out into Lake Michigan in a canoe."

Figure 14. Native Americans showed Louis Jolliet and Jacques Marquette a shortcut through the prairies between the Mississippi River and Lake Michigan via the Illinois, Des Plaines, and Chicago Rivers. (Adapted from a map by Tom Willcockson, in David Buisseret's *Historic Illinois from the Air* [Chicago: University of Chicago Press, 1990], 29. © 1990 by The University of Chicago.)

Figure 15. This photograph of a watercolor, possibly by Justin Herriott, ca. 1906, shows the Chicago River, from an eastern vantage point in 1830, being fed by the North Branch (on the right) and the South Branch (on the left), meeting at Wolf Point. A sandbar extends from the river mouth to Lake Michigan. Annotations on the photograph read: "1. Fort Dearborn; 2. Houses of Indian Traders; 3. Kinzie. First permanent resident; 4. Cobweb castle; 5. Streamlet through Randolph, Clark & State Sts.; 6. Cabin Russell E. Heacock built in 1827; 7. Streamlet through La Salle St.; 8. Streamlet through North Franklin St. and Burns Cabin; 9. Indian Chief Robinson; 10. Wolf Point; 11. Hardscrabble." (Courtesy of the Chicago Historical Society, ICHi 26982.)

Figure 16. Fort Dearborn and its surroundings, ca. 1832. Canal Commissioner Gurdon S. Hubbard, in his posthumously published autobiography, described the scene when he arrived in Chicago, several miles to the south of Fort Dearborn, in 1818: "The waving grass, intermingling with a rich profusion of wild flowers, was the most beautiful sight I had ever gazed upon. In the distance the grove of Blue Island loomed up, beyond it the timber on the Desplaines River. Looking north, I saw the whitewashed buildings of Fort Dearborn sparkling in the sunshine." (From a watercolor by Justin Herriott, ca. 1906. Courtesy of the Chicago Historical Society, P&S-1904.0034.)

his religion to the native people. In 1674 Marquette returned to the shores of Lake Michigan intent on establishing a mission at Kaskaskia, the "Grand Village" he encountered on the Illinois River. Weakened by illness, he wintered on the shores of "Mud Lake," a huge wetland west of Lake Michigan along the Chicago River. In the spring he traveled across the Chicago Portage along the prairie rivers and said Easter Mass at Kaskaskia. He died a month later en route to his home mission in Michigan.

Following in the footsteps of Marquette and Jolliet, Robert Cavalier Sieur de La Salle attempted to establish a trading empire centered in the Mississippi and Illinois River valleys in the 1680s. La Salle wrote that a canal "would be useless because the Des Plaines River is not navigable." He described a sandbar "at the mouth of the Chicago River . . . that not even a canoe [could] pass over" and how, because the prairies flooded during rains, it would be "very difficult to make and maintain a canal that does not immediately fill up with sand and gravel."

In spite of La Salle's apt assessment, the dream to build a canal to exploit the rich resources of the continent's interior persisted. In 1803 the federal government constructed Fort Dearborn to protect the mouth of the Chicago River and the Indian trading posts located there. Soldiers dug a channel through the sand bar, which was eventually destroyed in a massive federal harbor project.

In 1814, four years before Illinois gained statehood, President James Madison referred to the proposed route of the Illinois and Michigan Canal in his inaugural address: "How stupendous the idea! How dwindles the importance of the artificial canals of Europe compared to this water communication. If it should ever take place – and it is said the opening may be easily made – the [Illinois] Territory will become the seat of an immense commerce, and a market for the commodities of all regions." The initial surveys for the I&M route were conducted in 1816, but construction would not begin until 1836, after funds were raised and treaties were signed. Land granted by the federal government was auctioned to finance the canal.

Real estate speculation in Chicago was so intense that an English visitor, Harriet Martineau, wrote in *Society in America* that it was as though "some prevalent mania infected the whole people."

Following a series of financial reversals, the canal was completed in 1848. That April, when the first boat traveled from New Orleans to Buffalo via the I&M, the *Chicago Journal* proclaimed, "It was the wedding of the Father of Rivers to our inland seas – a union of the Mississippi with Lake Michigan; for the fruits of which union Chicago stands sponsor – COMMERCE is its first born – Agriculture and general prosperity its increase."

The Illinois and Michigan Canal created the first shipping highway between Lake Michigan and

the Mississippi River. It transformed the landscape, replacing the valley's prairies and wetlands with cities, towns, industry, and agriculture. Chicago boomed – both its population and exports quadrupled between 1848 and 1854 – and smaller towns along the canal route prospered as shipping points for the region's rich resources – stone, coal, and grain. Local industry, fueled by water power, helped canal towns become centers of employment and markets for meeting the needs of farmers.

The I&M was the last of the great American canals built during an era when waterways were the nation's major highways. The $6.4 million spent by the state of Illinois to build the 97-mile canal was a

Figure 17. A view of the Chicago River and the State Street Bridge, 1873, from a stereograph by Lovejoy and Foster. (Courtesy of the Chicago Historical Society, ICHi 00174.)

Figure 18. In 1871, when this engraving was featured in *Harper's Weekly*, the I&M Canal lock at Bridgeport was about to be removed as part of the plan to deepen the canal in an attempt to reverse the flow of the Chicago River and rid the lake of pollution. (Courtesy of the I&M Canal Collection, Lewis University.)

Figure 19. Thousands of Irish workers were recruited by contractors to dig the I&M Canal by hand. Housed in hastily built camps and shantytowns, the laborers were paid one dollar and a gill of whiskey for their fourteen- to fifteen-hour workdays. Working conditions were hard and sanitation was abysmal, leading to outbreaks of cholera and malaria. The men were often paid in canal scrip – issued by the state bank and worthless for anything but the redemption of canal land.

Figure 20. A river excursion boat, *The Belle of Ottawa*, from a stereograph by W. E. Bowman, ca. 1870. (Courtesy of James Jensen.)

Figure 21. Tall masted lake boats, canal boats filled with stone, barges carrying lumber, and a steam towboat fill this slip near Wolf Point. Lumberyards and grain elevators adjacent to the river are also served by the rails. (Photograph by John Gates, 1882. Courtesy of the Chicago Architectural Photographing Co., David R. Phillips.)

small percentage of the $200 million spent nationally between 1790 and 1860 to build a 3,325-mile canal network. By the mid-nineteenth century railroads were replacing canals as the major form of transportation. Soon the Illinois River valley was traversed by dozens of rail lines that competed with the canal for freight – rail lines that were located there to exploit the market created by the I&M. Despite competition, the canal continued to be the least expensive way to transport bulky goods like grain, lumber, and stone. Tonnage on the canal peaked in 1882 when over a million tons were shipped.

Figure 22. These old canal boats at Lockport were photographed ca. 1900–1905 from the decomposing boat (to the left) with weeds growing from its deck. By 1907 the Sanitary and Ship Canal had replaced the I&M Canal for most shipping east of Joliet. (Courtesy of the Detroit Photographic Collection, Library of Congress.)

Figure 23. Canal boats, like the one seen here in 1900, made Chicago the nation's grain capital. The city's first grain elevator was built in 1848, a year that also witnessed the founding of the Chicago Board of Trade. (Courtesy of the Metropolitan Water Reclamation District.)

Chicago's position as the commercial hub of the Midwest required continuous re-engineering of the landscape and waterways. The Canal Corridor is lined by generations of these improvements. Subsequent man-made waterways include the Sanitary and Ship Canal (1900; improved for transportation in 1906) and the Cal-Sag Channel (initiated in 1911, completed in 1922, and enlarged in 1955, when Lake Calumet became the terminus of the St. Lawrence Seaway). Rail lines proliferated with Chicago as

Figure 24. By the early 1940s the area where Fort Dearborn originally stood, to the right of the Michigan Avenue Bridge (seen open in this view), had become a vast commercial metropolis (see figs. 15–16). (Photograph by Carl Ulrich, ca. 1941. Courtesy of the Chicago Architectural Photographing Co., David R. Phillips.)

their focal point, while towns like Joliet and Blue Island offered secondary transfer points. In the twentieth century highways became dominant. Route 66 followed old Indian trails along Joliet Road, and today Interstates 55 and 80 move people and goods along the edges of the Canal Corridor. Midway Airport, built near the canal route in 1927, was the nation's busiest airport in the 1940s.

When ground was broken in Chicago in 1836 for the Illinois and Michigan Canal, the *Chicago*

Figure 25. The lock connecting the Chicago River to Lake Michigan is under construction in this 1937 aerial view. The Illinois Central Railroad yards are prominent south of the river. In addition to its economic pre-eminence, Chicago owes one of its greatest cultural amenities – its world-renowned lakefront parks – to the I&M Canal. In 1836 canal commissioners designated the lakefront on their plat as "Public Ground – A Common to Remain Forever Open, Clear and Free of any Buildings, or Other Obstruction whatever." (Photograph by Fred Sonne, Chicago Aerial Surveys. Courtesy of the Chicago Architectural Photographing Co., David R. Phillips.)

American proudly proclaimed: "This country is moving on like a young and healthy giant. The union of this chain of mighty lakes with the 'father of waters' removes all bounds to its growth and extent of commerce." The I&M realized Louis Jolliet's vision of a connection from the Great Lakes to the Gulf Coast 175 years after the explorer traveled the Chicago River. The Lake Michigan–Mississippi River connection ushered in the Midwest's transportation and industrial revolution and firmly established Chicago as the commercial gateway to the frontier. With the completion of the canal in 1848, the wetland located between the shores of Lake Michigan and the vast prairies to the west was destined to become one of the nation's greatest urban centers.

THE TRIANGLE

The Waterways That Built Chicago

CITY IN A WETLAND

The glacial meltwaters that carved the passage through the Illinois prairies left a huge marshy area around the shores of Lake Michigan. Early visitors to Chicago were simultaneously delighted by the promise of its location at the juncture of one of the Great Lakes and a waterway extending to the Mississippi and dismayed by its swampy conditions. In 1845 the Swedish pioneer Gustaf Unonius visited Chicago and later published a memoir in which he described the city as "with few exceptions resembling a trash can more than anything else [which] might best be likened to a vast mud puddle."

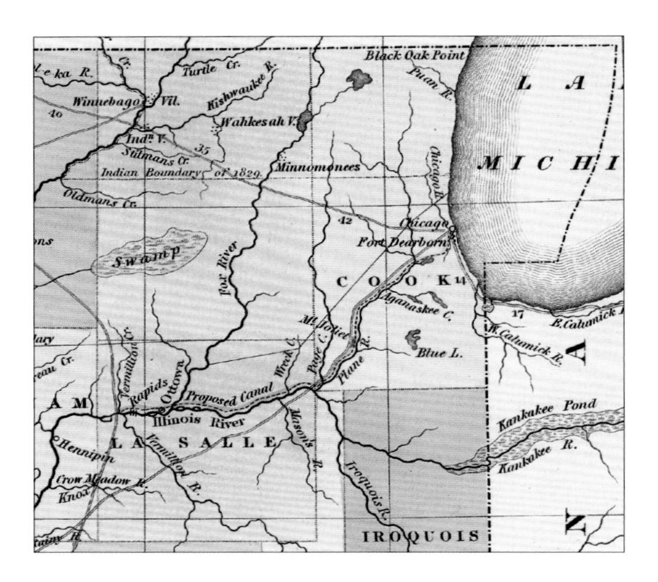

Figure 26. Detail from H. S. Tanner's "New Map of Illinois with its Proposed Canals, Roads and Distances from Place to Place along the Stage & Steam Boat Routes" (1833). The route of the "Proposed Canal," the I&M, is shown linking Lake Michigan to the Illinois River. Numerous swamps, sloughs, and small lakes are also visible on the map, reflecting the marshy character of the Chicago region. (Courtesy of the MacLean Collection.)

Beyond the muddy downtown area, a huge, twelve-square-mile swamp extended from the South Branch of the Chicago River to the Des Plaines River. Known as Mud Lake, this glacial depression was filled with water most of the year. The Chicago River was a sluggish stream flowing from Mud Lake (near the present intersection of 31st Street and Kedzie Avenue) northeast to Lake Michigan; its southern branch was navigable by lake boat from Bridgeport 5.5 miles to the lake. The marshy Des Plaines River flowed southwest from Mud Lake (near the present intersection of 47th Street and Harlem Avenue) into the Illinois River and the Mississippi watershed. A continental divide between the Chicago and Des Plaines Rivers was known as the Chicago Portage.

The first problem facing Chicago's investors and city builders was how to cut through the divide and make the natural passageway useful for shipping. The Illinois and Michigan Canal was the solution they devised. Starting in the early 1820s the state of Illinois tried repeatedly to organize itself for canal construction, creating and dissolving two commissions and a private stock company before the final commission was created in 1835. Proceeds from the sale of lands in downtown Chicago and along the canal route, granted to the state by the federal government, as well as loans from New York investors, ultimately allowed construction to begin. Ground was broken on July 4, 1836, in present-day Bridgeport, two miles east of Mud Lake.

Gurdon S. Hubbard supported construction of the canal as a state legislator and sought financing for it as a canal commissioner. He had crossed Mud Lake two decades earlier, in 1818, as an employee of the American Fur Company, and he used his closing address at the ground-breaking ceremony to recount his arduous journey.

It took Hubbard and his fellow fur traders three days to maneuver their empty boats across the lake, with four men on board pushing with poles and eight others wading in the mud jerking the boat along. In his posthumously published autobiography he offers this account:

The mud was very deep, and along the edge of the lake grew tall grass and wild rice, often reaching above a man's head, and so strong and dense it was almost impossible to walk through them. . . .

Those who waded through the mud frequently sank to their waist, and at times were forced to cling to the side of the boat to prevent going over their heads; after reaching the end and camping for the night came the task of ridding themselves from the blood suckers. The lake was full of these abominable black plagues, and . . . we were assailed by myriads of mosquitoes, that rendered sleep hopeless. . . . Those who had waded the lake suffered great agony, their limbs becoming swollen and inflamed. . . .

From the shores of Mud Lake the men continued along the future route of the Illinois and Michigan Canal to reach the trading post at Hennepin, just west of La Salle, the canal's eventual terminus. It took them three weeks to travel from the Des Plaines River to Starved Rock, carrying their goods on their backs while they dragged their lightened boats along the marshy, rocky waterway. When the canal opened in 1848, that arduous journey through the prairies was replaced by a day-long ride on a boat towed by mules.

Construction of the I&M required back-breaking labor, which was mostly supplied by Irish immigrants who were recruited by independent contractors in the East to dig the canal by hand. Dissatisfaction with working conditions and limited economic opportunities occasionally resulted in violent outbursts. Dissent was evident as early as

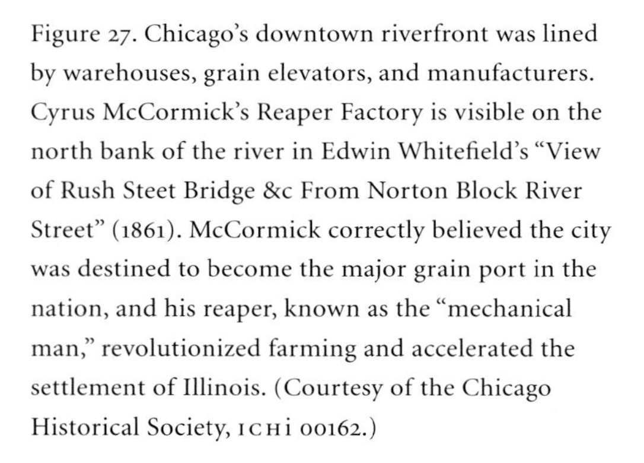
Figure 27. Chicago's downtown riverfront was lined by warehouses, grain elevators, and manufacturers. Cyrus McCormick's Reaper Factory is visible on the north bank of the river in Edwin Whitefield's "View of Rush Steet Bridge &c From Norton Block River Street" (1861). McCormick correctly believed the city was destined to become the major grain port in the nation, and his reaper, known as the "mechanical man," revolutionized farming and accelerated the settlement of Illinois. (Courtesy of the Chicago Historical Society, ICHi 00162.)

the ground-breaking ceremony. The *Chicago American* reported that as Hubbard and the other prominent citizens returned to the mouth of the river on a steamboat, a small group of Irishmen "stationing themselves at the stone quarry on the banks of the river, showered full volleys of stones amidst the thick crowd of ladies and gentlemen on the upper deck. The order was immediately given 'to land.' Some fifty passengers leaped ashore, some with bludgeons. . . . The assailants were soon led, covered with blood and wounds captive to the boat, where they were safely lodged in the hold, and brought into town. Thus ended the first campaign." Other incidents during the actual construction evidenced the workers' plight and fueled anti-Irish sentiment, including bloody feuds in Utica in 1838 and in Lockport in 1839.

On April 23, 1848, throngs gathered at the same site where ground had been broken in Bridgeport to greet the *General Thornton*, the first boat to travel the length of the new canal. One week later the *General Thornton* reached Buffalo with its shipment of sugar from New Orleans – a full two weeks before the first boat of the season arrived

in Buffalo from New York City via the Erie Canal. As the canal commissioners celebrated, U.S. Congressman Abraham Lincoln applauded the achievement in remarks on the floor of the House of Representatives.

THE NATION'S INLAND PORT

The Lake Michigan–Mississippi River commerce made possible by the canal established Chicago as the nation's largest inland port. During the I&M's first operating season in 1848, shipments of corn from Chicago to the East increased eightfold and lumber receipts doubled. Grain, stone, and coal from the canal region and sugar, molasses, coffee, and other products from the New Orleans and St. Louis markets were carried to Chicago and then shipped north and east. St. Louis's grain receipts declined dramatically as a direct result of the canal opening. In 1868 more than twenty-six thousand vessels arrived in Chicago, exceeding the combined totals for San Francisco, New Orleans, and New York.

The crowded Chicago River was lined with grain elevators, warehouses, and industry. Extending west and south along the river from downtown, and concentrated near the canal's opening in the Bridgeport and Pilsen neighborhoods, were huge lumberyards. The "city of lumber" stored along the river and canal came from the gigantic forests of Wisconsin and was used to build Chicago and the prairie settlements to the west. In 1865 the Union Stockyards were created, making Chicago the center of the meat-packing industry. The southern fork of the South Branch of the Chicago River, which joined the river near Ashland Avenue, next to the site where the I&M branched off to the southwest, gained the name Bubbly Creek because stockyard workers dumped their refuse into the water and bubbles were produced as the carcasses decomposed.

Chicago's port was also served by the burgeoning railroads. The first railroad company laid track in Chicago in 1848, in 1856 the first railroad bridged the Mississippi River, and by 1860 Chicago was the focus of ten trunk lines with close to three thousand miles of track. Fifty-eight passenger trains and thirty-eight freight trains arrived and departed daily. Nevertheless, the canal continued to be the

Figure 28. Bridges spanned the Chicago River at every north-south street in the downtown area. Technical innovation was required to create movable bridges, as pictured in this detail of the Clark Street swing bridge, that would limit the disruptions to both river and street traffic. Chicago's first movable bridge, a wooden drawbridge, was built in 1834 but was replaced in 1840 by a floating bridge hinged to the bank at Clark Street. In 1856 the first iron swing bridge was installed at Rush Street, rotating on a pier in the middle of the river (figs. 17 and 27). Subsequent innovations include the vertical lift bridge (pl. 16), the Scherzer rolling lift bridge (pl. 15), and the double-leaf trunnion bascule bridge, which can be raised and lowered in less than a minute (pls. 4, 10, and 12). Today Chicago has forty-seven movable bridges – more than any other city in the world. (Photograph taken in 1929. Courtesy of the Chicago Architectural Photographing Co., David R. Phillips.)

Figure 29. Railroads, seen here in 1905 along the Chicago River, came to Chicago in 1848 and followed the same route as the newly opened canal. (Courtesy of the Metropolitan Water Reclamation District.)

least expensive way to transport bulk goods. It gave Chicago an advantage over railroad towns like St. Louis – even after the railroads gained prominence – because by competing with trains the I&M kept Chicago's freight prices low.

PURIFYING THE WATER

Chicago's rapid expansion brought predictable urban problems, not the least of which was the maintenance of a clean water supply. In 1855 the city gained national attention when it built a new sewer system on top of the streets and then raised the streets and buildings out of the mud to accommodate the pipes. Unfortunately the new sewers drained into the Chicago River, which flowed into Lake Michigan, thereby polluting the city's water supply. As the river became even more contaminated, freshwater intakes were moved farther and farther out into the lake in a series of unsuccessful efforts

Figure 30. When the I&M Canal, shown here in 1917, looking east from the California Avenue Bridge, was replaced by the Sanitary and Ship Canal, its bed in Chicago was still used for transportation purposes: first for rail lines and later as the right-of-way for the Adlai E. Stevenson Expressway. (Courtesy of the Chicago Historical Society, ICHi 27021.)

Figure 31. Construction began on Interstate 55, known in Chicago as the Stevenson Expressway, in 1957. The new highway was built on the first seven miles of the bed of the I&M Canal and connected Chicago with St. Louis and New Orleans.

to end frequent epidemics of cholera, typhoid, and dysentery that killed thousands of people.

To address this massive public health problem, the city of Chicago and the canal commissioners decided to deepen the Illinois and Michigan Canal, causing it to draw water from the lake into the river and reversing the river's flow from east to west. This "deep cut," completed in 1871, had originally been proposed in 1836 but was abandoned for the less-expensive construction of a pumping station and several feeder canals. On July 15, just three months before the Great Chicago Fire, the I&M Canal lock at Bridgeport was removed and a celebration hailed the new engineering wonder. A con-

temporary remarked that "the horrible, black, stinking river of a few weeks ago . . . has since become clear enough for fish to live in, by reason of the deepening of the canal which draws to the Mississippi a perpetual flow of pure water from Lake Michigan."

Fluctuating lake and river levels limited the efficacy of this solution, and in 1879 severe flooding caused the Chicago River to flow east again, discharging into the lake for thirty days. In 1882 the pumping station and lock were rebuilt at Bridgeport to limit the reverse flow of water toward the lake during rainstorms. Several years later the inadequacy of the canal to dilute and carry away the city's sewage was emphasized when extremely heavy rains again caused the Des Plaines River to overflow into the Chicago River. The sewage that consequently poured into Lake Michigan produced a deadly outbreak of cholera. By 1891 the typhoid death rate in the city had reached 174 per 100,000, the highest of any city in the civilized world.

Starting in 1879 the Citizens Association of Chicago began to advocate for construction of a larger canal comparable in size to the Chicago River. In 1889 the Sanitary District Enabling Act was passed by the state legislature to create the Sanitary District of Chicago (now known as the Metropolitan Water Reclamation District) to build a canal big enough to divert the wastewater from the entire city, which by then had a population of

1.7 million. On September 3, 1892, after the completion of extensive engineering studies, construction began on the Sanitary and Ship Canal (originally known as the Drainage Canal). In an act of what the historian Donald Miller has called "heroic chutzpah," Chicago prepared to permanently reverse the flow of the Chicago River and transport its sewage westward, diluting it with lake water as it flowed into the Des Plaines River valley.

The new canal extended twenty-eight miles from Chicago to Lockport; it was 25 feet deep and 160 feet wide at its narrowest point – bigger than the Suez Canal in Egypt. Construction of the Sanitary Canal represented the largest earth-moving project in the world at the time. To build it, excavating machines had been invented that would also be used fifteen years later to construct the Panama Canal.

Portions of the Chicago River itself were enlarged as well. An embankment built across the entrance to the Des Plaines River valley diverted that river to a new channel, leaving the old Mud Lake permanently dry. Butterfly- and bear-trap dams and gigantic waste gates were installed to prevent flooding south of the canal. The Sanitary Canal's floor is at the same level as the bottom of

Figure 32. Workers on the Sanitary and Ship Canal, ca. 1895. (Courtesy of the Chicago Historical Society, ICHi 27248.)

Figure 33. The Metropolitan Water Reclamation District constructed a Sidestream Elevated Pool Aeration station (SEPA) at the confluence of the Sanitary and Ship Canal and the Cal-Sag Channel. In addition to purifying the waterways by adding oxygen to them, the station was designed to create an attractive park (see fig. 34 and pls. 25–26).

Figure 34. The Sanitary and Ship Canal, on the left, meets the Cal-Sag Channel, on the right, just past a rise known to geologists as Mount Forest Island. This glacial island now contains the 14,000-acre Palos and Sag Valley Forest Preserves, first established by Cook County in 1914 on land that had served as Native American winter retreats and poor-quality farms given to Irish canal workers in lieu of pay. The remnants of the giant Saganashkee Slough are visible on the right. This and other sloughs make the forest preserves major destinations for bird watchers to observe migrating water fowl. SEPA Station No. 5 (see fig. 33) is visible at the confluence. Just past it, parallel to the Sanitary and Ship Canal and intersecting the Cal-Sag Channel, is the I&M Canal (see also pls. 25–26).

the Niagara River in New York, so these structures confined water all the way from Niagara Falls.

It took a workforce of 8,500 men to build the Sanitary and Ship Canal, most of them newly arrived immigrants. Chicago and Lemont neighborhoods expanded dramatically as a result. This was also the first time that African Americans migrated to Chicago in large numbers from the southern United States to work on a construction project.

On January 2, 1900, the main channel of the Sanitary Canal was opened and the Chicago River's flow was reversed. Governmental bodies in

St. Louis, Joliet, and Peoria had unsuccessfully tried to prevent the opening of the canal, afraid of pollution from Chicago's sewage. The Illinois and Michigan Canal commissioners had also fought the new canal, justly fearing that it would reduce the I&M's water supply and compete with its commercial abilities. While the Sanitary Canal was not originally used for shipping, between 1906 and 1908 it was made navigable by extending it about a mile south of Lockport and adding a single lock to accommodate the forty-foot drop between Lockport and Joliet. By this time the new canal had brought about a marked improvement in health conditions in Chicago, the typhoid death rate dropping by 91 percent as of 1908.

THE SECOND PORT OF CHICAGO: THE CAL-SAG CHANNEL

The shores of Lake Michigan around the mouth of the Calumet River, where a Potawatomi burial ground once stood, developed early as a fishing settlement. This area was familiar to travelers from the east who entered Chicago by road. In 1822 Gurdon S. Hubbard abandoned the portage route through the Chicago Outlet Valley and created a trail going south from State Street in Chicago, across the Calumet River and the town of Blue Island, southwest into present-day Will County, and extending all the way to Native American hunting grounds in Danville, Indiana. In 1827 he gave up fur trading and became Chicago's first meat packer, driving hogs into the city along "Hubbard's Trail."

By the 1850s the small town of Ainsworth emerged near the mouth of the Calumet River; it would later become the Chicago neighborhood known as South Chicago. Lake Calumet, located west of the shoreline, was three miles square, offering a natural harbor and docking facility. Slightly southwest along the Little Calumet River the community of Portland developed in what is now Blue Island, on the highest point in Cook County – a limestone outcropping that was among the first land to re-emerge when glacial Lake Chicago began its slow subsidence. A 16.8-mile feeder canal to the I&M was constructed in Blue Island in 1849, supplying water to the Illinois and Michigan Canal from the Little Calumet River.

Figure 35. In the nineteenth century a community known as Sag, or Sag Bridge, grew up at the high point of Mount Forest Island, surrounding St. James of the Sag Church (see pl. 28). The church is all that remains of the settlement of Sag. This grave is the oldest surviving marked grave in Cook County, that of Michael Dillon, probably a canal worker, who died in 1846.

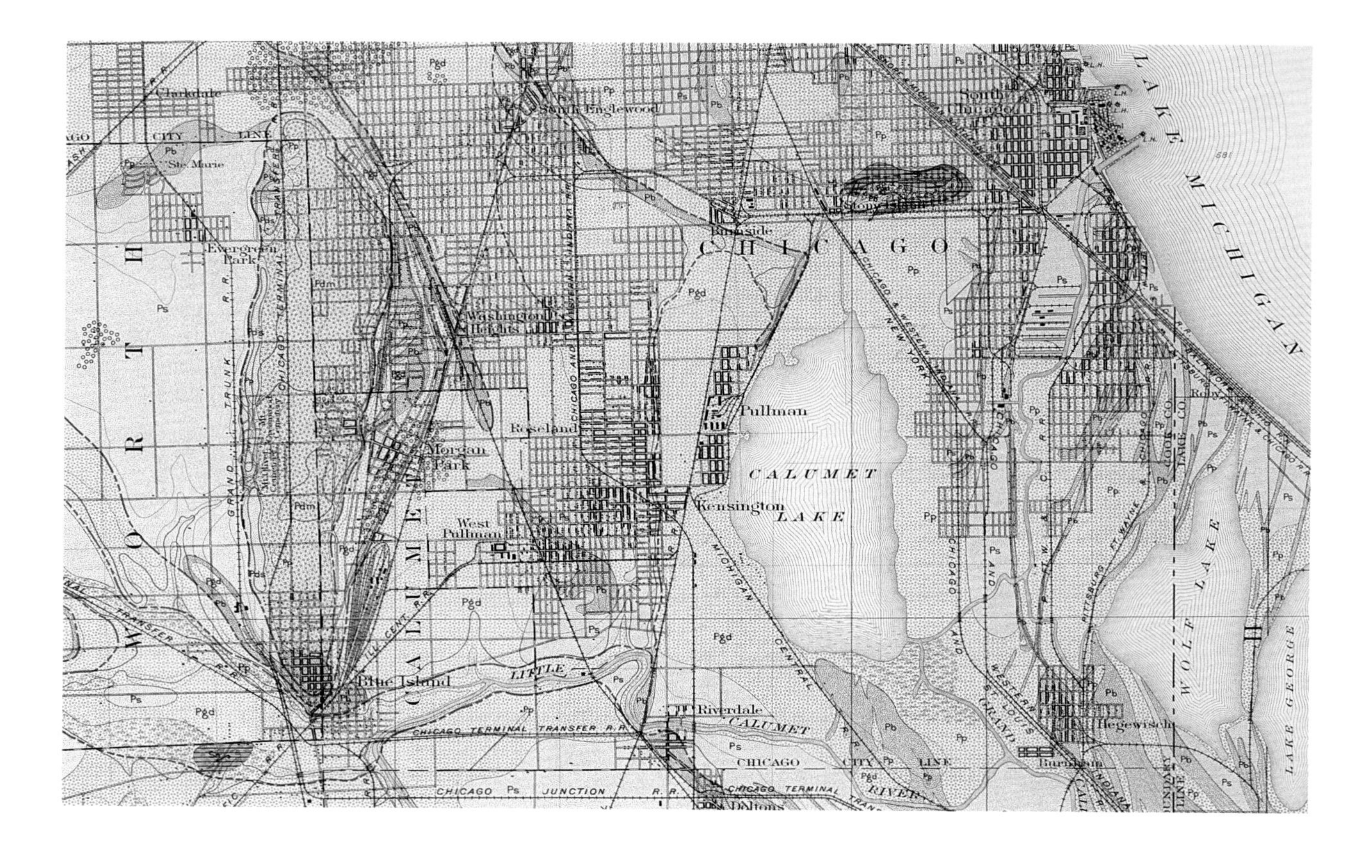

Figure 36. This detail of Calumet Lake, which has since been partially filled in, is taken from the "Chicago Quadrangle Map" (1902), made before the construction of the Cal-Sag Channel. It also shows the meandering Grand and Little Calumet Rivers. The Cal-Sag began at a set of locks constructed near the bend in the Little Calumet River, just west of Riverdale and the Illinois Central Railroad tracks. (Courtesy of the MacLean Collection.)

In 1869 the U.S. Congress appropriated a quarter of a million dollars to improve the Calumet River and its harbor in partnership with the private Calumet Canal and Dock Company. The region around Lake Calumet developed rapidly after the Great Chicago Fire of 1871 stimulated industries to locate away from the downtown area. Served by railroads and the new port, the Calumet region was an ideal location for heavy industry. In 1875 the Brown Steel and Iron Company opened a mill on the Calumet River; five years later the North Chicago Rolling Mill Company located its new plant, the South Works, at the river's mouth. Steel mills proliferated, and between 1872 and 1892 ore imports increased fifteenfold. European immigrants moved to the neighborhoods around the steel mills in droves and soon were employed by other diversifying industries as well.

Across from the steel mills at Lake Calumet was Pullman, a model company town developed

in 1881 by George Pullman to produce railroad sleeping cars. Internationally renowned as an example of modern urban planning, the town, designed by the architect Solon S. Beman, eventually housed twelve thousand workers. Pullman's paternalistic practices, initially hailed as farsighted, would ultimately engender violent labor strife, leading up to the notorious Pullman Strike of 1894.

In 1906 shipping on the Calumet River equaled that of the Chicago River; ten years later Calumet River shipping was ahead by 500 percent. With rail lines crisscrossing the communities of South Chicago and Blue Island, the former became a world-renowned center of the steel industry while the latter became a rail hub.

In 1911 construction began on yet another canal, one that would link the Sanitary and Ship Canal to a second port on Lake Michigan: Chicago's newer South Side port at Calumet Harbor. The Cal-Sag Channel was also originally intended as a sanitary canal, designed to pull lake water through the Little Calumet and Calumet Rivers and feed the water and its sewage into the Sanitary Canal. The Cal-Sag joined the Sanitary Canal at a point southwest of the Chicago Portage known as "the Sag." (The word *sag* abbreviates the Native American word *saganashkee*, thought to mean "slush of the earth.") The Saganashkee Slough was a wetland at the headwaters of the Calumet River, on the edge of Mount Forest Island, which was the highest point in glacial Lake Chicago. The island is still visible as a rise between the Cal-Sag Channel and the Sanitary and Ship Canal (see fig. 34 and pl. 25).

When it was completed in 1922 the Cal-Sag provided a dependable shipping channel between the modern port of Chicago and the Sanitary and Ship Canal – and thus the Illinois and Mississippi river system. In 1933 the Cal-Sag and the Sanitary Canal became part of a modern shipping network, completely replacing the I&M Canal as the connection between Lake Michigan and the Mississippi. The I&M was closed that year when the U.S. Army Corps of Engineers completed the Illinois Waterway, which channelized the Illinois River all the way to its juncture with the Mississippi.

Figure 37. Prior to the infamous strike of 1894, the planned community of Pullman was one of Chicago's proudest accomplishments. This panorama of Pullman comes from a souvenir album issued by Chisholm Bros. of Portland, Maine, who manufactured "Chas. Frey's Original Souvenir Albums of all American & Canadian Cities and Sceneries," ca. 1892. (Courtesy of Gerald W. Adelmann.)

Figure 38. The modern port of Chicago is entered through the mouth of the Calumet River, which flows past the working-class neighborhood of South Chicago, shown here in an aerial view of the Calumet River and Lake Michigan (see pl. 38).

The most recent chapter in the history of the inland waterway link across the old Chicago Portage occurred in the 1950s, when the St. Lawrence Seaway from the Atlantic Ocean was built with Calumet Harbor as its terminus. The seaway made it possible for oceangoing ships to travel the inland waters of North America.

In anticipation of the seaway's completion, the Cal-Sag Channel was enlarged in 1955, and Lake Calumet was developed as the most comprehensive terminal complex on the Great Lakes. In June 1959 the royal yacht *Britannia*, carrying Queen Elizabeth II and Prince Philip, led a procession of fifty vessels from Montreal to Chicago to herald the new opportunities for international commerce.

The neighborhoods around the Calumet River were strongholds of industrial workers for a century, until the recession of the 1970s took its toll on the steel industry. While a variety of industries in the region survive, the closure of the giant Wisconsin Steel and South Works caused widespread unemployment and decline in the 1980s and early 1990s. The city and community residents are now seeking new uses for the "brown fields" left by the steel plants; in the process they are also discovering remnants of ancient ecosystems and pouring energy into a new local conservation movement. The remains of the Pullman plant have been acquired by the Illinois Historic Preservation Agency, which will develop a museum featuring both the railroad industry and the nation's first planned industrial community. The National Park Service is studying creation of what could become the Calumet National Ecological Park. This new kind of partnership park would model itself on concepts pioneered by the Illinois and Michigan Canal National Heritage Corridor to celebrate and protect the historic and natural resources that survive alongside vast industries throughout the entire Lake Calumet area.

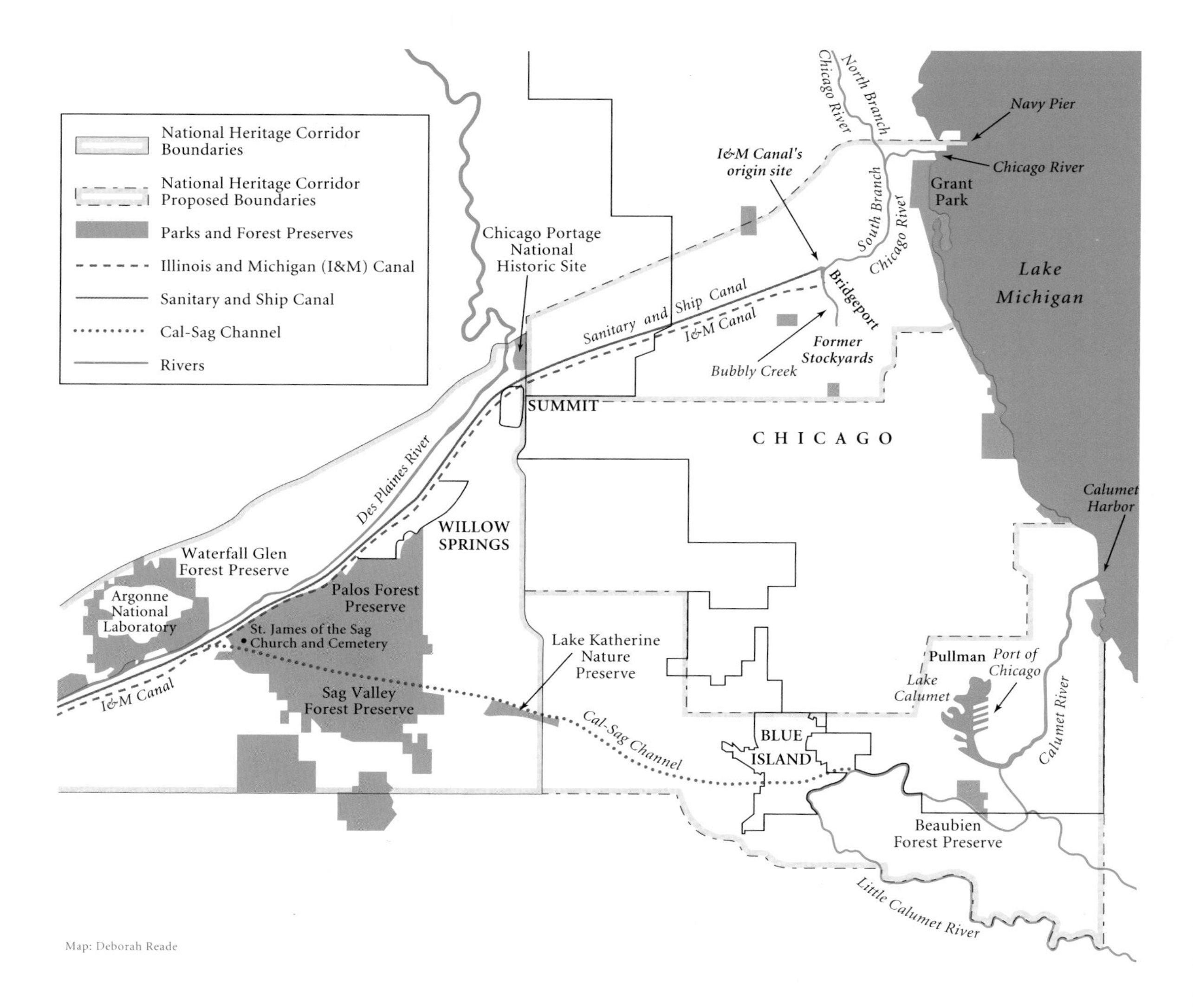

PORTFOLIO PLATES

PLATE 7. Early settlers likened the "inland sea" of Lake Michigan to the vast, oceanic prairies.

PLATE 8. This algae-covered water is a rare survivor of the marshy landscape that greeted Chicago's first settlers. The Chicago Portage National Historic Site contains the last remains of the huge swampy area called Mud Lake.

PLATE 9. The vision of Chicago as a vast commercial metropolis that originated with Louis Jolliet was embraced by the nation's leaders in the early 1800s and captivated builders and speculators in the 1830s. The Sears Tower, at the western edge of Chicago's downtown, serves as a landmark in many of Edward Ranney's photographs.

PLATE 10. In this photograph the Michigan Avenue Bridge is elevated for repairs. Today the Chicago River is quiet, since the port of Chicago has shifted south to Lake Calumet. The city is distinguished by its nineteenth- and twentieth-century skyscrapers, including the white terra cotta Wrigley Building seen on the right.

PLATE 11. This double-leaf bascule bridge, located roughly at the site of Fort Dearborn, was instrumental in opening Chicago's North Side to commercial development in the 1920s. During a 1992 repair the counterweights malfunctioned and the bridge "fell up," damaging the structure.

PLATE 12. This double-trunnion bascule bridge was built in 1913. The Civic Opera Building, constructed in 1929 to house the Lyric Opera, stands to the right of the bridge.

PLATE 13. Since its founding as a canal town, Chicago has been in a constant state of change. Despite the demolition of some of its historic structures, the city is increasing its efforts to preserve its landmarks.

PLATE 14. By the late 1800s Chicago was America's rail center, a fact that shaped the local landscape. Rail yards prevented the city's growth to the south and inspired the construction of skyscrapers to maximize the density of the central core.

PLATE 15. The Cermak Road Bridge, which opened in 1906, is the last remaining functional Scherzer rolling lift bridge. Its huge rocking counterweights are shown here. The city is in the process of rehabilitating the bridge in recognition of its landmark stature.

PLATE 16. This vertical lift bridge, built in 1914, is raised and lowered by steel cables connected to counterweights that fall as the lift span rises. No longer operated manually from the bridgetender's house, it is now monitored off-site by video camera and controlled by automated equipment.

PLATE 17. At the turning basin, located near the 2800 block of South Ashland Avenue, the South Branch of the Chicago River joins the Sanitary and Ship Canal, shown here extending west on the left. To the right (south) is the southern fork of the South Branch, known as Bubbly Creek. The I&M Canal joined the river here, and the small triangular spit of land visible between Bubbly Creek and the Chicago River is all that is left of the busy canal landing. The structures in the foreground will soon be replaced by a new printing plant for the *Chicago Sun-Times* (see figs. 2–3).

PLATE 18. In 1907 the U.S. Army Corps of Engineers dredged a turning basin on the Chicago River in the area where goods were originally transferred from lake boats to the I&M Canal. This photograph was taken from the site of the canal landing at Ashland Avenue, where an interpretive park is planned.

PLATE 19. Located east of the turning basin, this house recalls the residences built for laborers who settled in Bridgeport in the mid-1800s.

PLATE 20. Refuse from the stockyards was dumped into the river, and bubbles produced by the decomposing carcasses gave Bubbly Creek its name.

PLATE 21. Today the Chicago River is used primarily by recreational boats, stored in dry dock during the winter.

PLATE 22. The overgrowth and marshy conditions of the Des Plaines River backwater are reminiscent of the dense natural growth described by fur traders who made their way across Mud Lake in the early 1800s.

PLATE 23. The site where Louis Jolliet and Fr. Jacques Marquette, as well as subsequent traders, portaged over a continental divide between the Chicago and Des Plaines Rivers is visible in the wooded foreground, to the east of the Des Plaines backwater. The Sanitary and Ship Canal on the right replaced the Chicago River in this area. Its construction relocated the Des Plaines River and drained Mud Lake.

PLATE 24. Willow Springs, about sixteen miles from Chicago's lakefront, is the first place where the three waterways can be observed running parallel to each other. The Cook County Forest Preserve has developed a nine-mile bicycle trail along the I&M Canal in Willow Springs.

PLATE 25. This aerial view of the point where the Sanitary and Ship Canal (left) and the Cal-Sag Channel (right) come together shows the glacial area known as Mount Forest Island. The I&M Canal is the small waterway that, in this view, runs parallel to the right of the Sanitary Canal and ends at the Cal-Sag (see fig. 34). The Des Plaines River is seen to the left of the Sanitary Canal.

PLATE 26. The ridge visible beyond the junkyards is all that remains of Mount Forest Island, the highest point to rise out of glacial Lake Chicago more than nine thousand years ago.

PLATE 27. The channel was built between 1911 and 1922 to bring sewage from the Calumet Harbor industrial region into the Sanitary Canal. It was widened in the 1950s and is still used for shipping.

PLATE 28. Canal and quarry workers settled in the area in the 1830s. The church, made of local dolomite, was built in 1859 and later modified. The graveyard contains monuments commemorating early settlers, including the oldest surviving marked grave in Cook County (see fig. 35).

PLATE 29. Blue Island developed around the feeder canal and dam completed in 1849 to bring water from the Little Calumet River 16.8 miles to the I&M Canal. By 1913 Blue Island had four railroad systems and two belt lines, making connections to all the rail lines in Chicago.

PLATE 30. Sidestream Elevated Pool Aeration stations were constructed along the Cal-Sag Channel to increase the oxygen content of the waterway. These award-winning stations were also designed as public parks to provide access to the waterfront.

PLATE 31. Named for George Pullman's daughter, this hotel was the architectural showpiece of the planned community of Pullman. Recently acquired by the state, it is open for Sunday brunch and tours.

PLATE 32. When streets were raised to accommodate citywide drainage improvements, the results did not always conform with older building designs, as evidenced here.

PLATE 33. Built at the mouth of the Calumet River in 1880, the U. S. Steel Works eventually grew to occupy 575 acres and employ some twelve thousand workers. Massive layoffs beginning in the 1970s concluded with the plant closing its doors by 1992.

PLATE 34. Acme Steel is one of the few surviving steel works in the Lake Calumet–Cal-Sag Channel area. The huge conveyor shown here was designed to move coke from the storage area across the Calumet River to the blast furnaces.

PLATE 35. The blast furnaces are on the left. In the distance, to the east (right), is a tree-lined residential neighborhood.

PLATE 36. The waterways continue to be the least-expensive way to ship bulky goods like gravel and sand, seen in the foreground, and grain, represented by the elevator in the background.

PLATE 37. The bridge beyond the salt pile is the Ewing Avenue Bridge at the mouth of the Calumet River (see fig. 38 and pl. 38).

PLATE 38. This vertical lift railroad bridge frames the mouth of the Calumet River. Ships traveling the St. Lawrence Seaway enter the Calumet Harbor area here. Junked cars are crushed and recycled at the plant dominated by cranes to the right (see pl. 37).

7. Lake Michigan, looking south from the lake lock at the mouth of the Chicago River.

8. *Backwater of the Des Plaines River at the Chicago Portage National Historic Site.*

9. *Chicago and Lake Michigan, looking northeast from the sixty-sixth floor of the Sears Tower.*

10. *Chicago River and Michigan Avenue Bridge, seen from the Columbus Street Bridge.*

11. *Michigan Avenue Bridge undergoing repairs.*

12. *Chicago River at the Washington Street Bridge, looking east.*

13. *Demolition of the Marshall Field River Warehouse (Burnham and Co., 1904), looking north from Polk Street.*

14. *Amtrak Yards from 18th Street, looking north.*

15. *Cermak Road Bridge and counterweight, South Branch of the Chicago River.*

16. *Chicago River and railroad bridge, seen from the Canal Street Bridge.*

17. *I&M Canal's origin site and the Chicago River turning basin, looking northeast toward downtown Chicago.*

18. *Turning basin on the Chicago River, from the I&M Canal's origin site looking northeast.*

19. *Lock Street in Bridgeport, looking north to Chicago's Loop.*

20. *Bubbly Creek, near the former Union Stockyards, looking south.*

21. *Crowley's Yacht Yard.*

22. *Overgrowth at the Chicago Portage National Historic Site.*

23. *View from the Chicago Portage National Historic Site, looking east to Chicago.*

24. Des Plaines River, Sanitary and Ship Canal, I&M Canal and bicycle trail, looking north from Willow Springs Road Bridge.

25. *Confluence of the Sanitary and Ship Canal and the Cal-Sag Channel, looking northeast.*

26. *Palos Ridge and automobile junkyards at Route 171, north of Lemont.*

27. Cal-Sag Channel with river tow and barge in the Palos Forest Preserve.

28. *St. James of the Sag Church and Cemetery.*

29. *Railroad bridges over the Cal-Sag Channel near Blue Island.*

30. *SEPA Station No. 4 on the Cal-Sag Channel near Worth.*

31. *Hotel Florence, Pullman.*

32. *Housing on Burley Avenue at 91st Street, South Chicago.*

33. *Former U.S. Steel Works, Calumet Harbor.*

34. *Acme Steel Company and conveyor, Chicago.*

35. *Acme Steel Company, from atop the conveyor, Chicago.*

36. *Acme Steel Company storage area and the Calumet River, looking southwest, Chicago.*

37. Road salt pile near Calumet Harbor.

38. *Barge and vertical lift bridge in Calumet Harbor, seen from Ewing Avenue looking toward Lake Michigan.*

LEMONT TO JOLIET

Canal Towns in the River Valley

Figure 39. In 1847 Boston Courier reporter J. H. Buckingham wrote of the Illinois River valley, depicted in this ca. 1910 postcard: "The whole road from Chicago lies through a tract of country which is a sort of valley – if you can call that a valley where there are no hills on either side – which was once evidently the bed of a river. The prairie is in many places undulating, or rolling, and the waters of Lake Michigan once undoubtedly flowed uninterruptedly through to the Illinois [R]iver." (Courtesy of Lewis University.)

SETTLING THE VALLEY

Just outside Chicago's dense urban environment, the Canal Corridor is clearly a valley. Canal towns nestle along bluffs that become progressively steeper as the Des Plaines and Illinois Rivers descend toward the Mississippi. When the canal opened in 1848, the *Joliet Signal* quoted a citizen's celebratory speech: "With a soil unrivaled for fertility – a genial climate – inexhaustible supplies of coal and stone – water power abundant to manufacture . . . a landscape whose beauties challenge the world for a parallel, and [the I&M Canal,] a line of improvement that connects us with the broad ocean and the world, what country can rival ours!"

Canal towns evolved as local transfer points for grain and other farm products and as quarrying, mining, milling, and manufacturing centers. Connections between Chicago business interests and canal towns surface repeatedly. Examples include Gurdon S. Hubbard, who invested in the Marseilles Manufacturing Company; John Armour, the owner of the Seneca Grain Elevator and the brother of George Armour, who owned an elevator ten times the size of Seneca's on the banks of the Chicago River; and W. D. Boyce, an Ottawa resident who founded the Boy Scouts of America in 1910 and was a Chicago newspaper publisher and real estate developer who milled his paper in Marseilles.

THE DES PLAINES RIVER VALLEY

Three towns in the Des Plaines River valley – Lockport, Lemont, and Joliet – grew and prospered as a result of the Illinois and Michigan Canal. Canal commissioners made Lockport their headquarters. Lemont evolved as a quarrying center after the canal was completed, and Joliet prospered as the biggest Canal Corridor town outside Chicago when it became a secondary hub for the railroads that followed the canal.

Lemont grew dramatically in the 1890s to serve the thousands of immigrants who came to build the Sanitary and Ship Canal. When the canal was completed, Lockport lost the prominence it had gained as the headquarters for the I&M Canal, but its improved shipping capacity and the availability of large tracts of land nearby made it attractive to a new kind of industry: Texaco located the corridor's first petroleum refinery in Lockport in 1911.

The I&M needed five locks to negotiate a forty-foot drop in elevation between Lockport and Joliet; the new Sanitary and Ship Canal used only one. The 2.65-mile extension of the Sanitary Canal to Joliet was completed in 1907, with a temporary lock opened at Lockport in 1908 and a permanent lock completed in 1910, making obsolete the first thirty-three miles of the I&M, from Bridgeport to Joliet.

Figure 40. For most of its length the I&M Canal was sixty feet wide, but widewaters, like the one shown here in Lockport, ca. 1880, were strategically located to allow canal boat crews to transfer goods. When the canal opened in 1848, W. E. Little Esq. of Joliet, writing in the *Joliet Signal*, credited the citizens of Lockport with "having launched and started the first boat to be employed for purposes of Navigation on the Illinois and Michigan canal . . . a main connecting link between the west and the east. . . . How magnificent will be the union!" (Courtesy of Gerald W. Adelmann.)

Lockport had been a strategic site for water power since 1848, when the I&M Canal commissioners constructed the Hydraulic Basin, with a twenty-one-foot fall of water. The basin was used by the entrepreneur Hiram Norton to power flour, lumber, and paper mills. In 1907 the forty-foot drop in the water level between Lockport and Joliet was used to power a hydroelectric plant on the Sanitary and Ship Canal that is still operated by the Metropolitan Water Reclamation District. In the 1930s this waterway became part of the Illinois Waterway,

39. *Sanitary and Ship Canal and the Des Plaines River, looking north from the northern edge of Joliet.*

extending the Sanitary Canal's shipping capacity to the Mississippi.

CANAL TOWNS AS COMMERCIAL CENTERS

Downtown Lemont, Lockport, and Joliet were vibrant community centers, offering shopping, banking, entertainment, food, lodging, and public services to residents of the region. Townspeople walked downtown to transact business, reach the canal or the train, attend school and religious services, and meet their neighbors. Farmers' wagons crowded the streets while their owners traded grain, sold produce, and purchased goods and services.

Grain elevators dotted the landscape of all the canal towns, often serving both the railroads and the canal. The elevators were the primary link between local farms and the international commerce made possible by the canal. Lockport was the center of the Canal Corridor's mid-nineteenth-century grain trade and also boasted the largest flour-milling complex in Illinois.

A farmer who delivered grain to an elevator received a receipt redeemable for an equal quantity of the same grade grain. Grain could easily be traded by exchanging these receipts, often at the Chicago Board of Trade. Retailers and other entrepreneurs accepted elevator receipts for barter, establishing themselves as grain traders in the process. While the flow of grain was primarily from west to east along the canal and the railroads, grain and other commodities were also shipped between towns along the canal.

Plate 39. The black railroad lift bridge at the center of this aerial view marks the juncture of the Des Plaines River and the Sanitary Canal. The Lockport power plant and forty-foot lock are visible beyond the bridge. The I&M Canal is visible to the east (right) of the railroad yards.

Figure 41. The Lockport Power Plant is visible to the left of the lock in this photograph taken in April 1907, eight months before the extension of the Sanitary and Ship Canal to Joliet was completed. (Courtesy of the Metropolitan Water Reclamation District.)

Figure 42. This long view of Sanitary Canal construction in Lockport was taken in February 1906 before the power plant was completed. (Courtesy of the Metropolitan Water Reclamation District.)

HOT
CHILLI
CON
CARNE
OUR OWN MAKE.
10¢
CIGARS
MITCHELL'S
RESTAURANT
& QUICK LUNCH
CAFE
MITCHELL'S
SPECIAL SANDWICH 15¢

QUARRYING

Lockport, Lemont, and Joliet also evolved as centers of the stone quarrying industry. During construction of the I&M Canal, dolomite bedrock was discovered close to the surface in the Des Plaines River valley. This dolomite, known as Lemont or Joliet limestone, has a high level of magnesium that gives it a warm yellow color. A sedimentary rock created by the Silurian sea that covered this portion of the continent 400 million years ago, dolomite was first quarried to build the canal locks and walls using a drill patented by a Lockport inventor, Isaac Merit Singer, who would go on to invent the sewing machine.

After the canal's completion, at least fifty quarries opened in the Des Plaines River valley between Sag and Joliet. Workers produced flagstone, crushed stone, and dimension stone for buildings. The quarrying industry attracted thousands of immigrants to Lemont, Lockport, and Joliet, especially after the Great Chicago Fire of 1871 created a tremendous demand for stone. Germans and Swedes were later joined by Poles, Bohemians, and Italians. In 1885, and again in 1893, strikes over wages led to violent clashes.

Chicago and the canal towns were filled with buildings and sidewalks made of dolomite. Numerous examples of residential and commercial architecture that include this local stone survive in Lemont, Lockport, and Joliet. Among Chicago's remaining dolomite buildings are the Water Tower and Pumping Station, which survived the Great Fire of 1871 and are landmarks on North Michigan Avenue.

Figure 43. H. H. Carter, a pharmacist and amateur photographer, created an unusual record of life in downtown Lockport. Many of the buildings visible in these ca. 1915 photographs survive in the downtown area. (Courtesy of P. H. Ogren.)

Figure 44. Jonathan "Styx" MacDonald, a local newspaper publisher, philosopher, and artist, painted this view of Lockport ca. 1880, when Tenth and State Streets were still unpaved. The Norton Warehouse and portions of the mills beyond it are visible in the background. (Courtesy of Gerald W. Adelmann.)

Figure 45. The Norton Warehouse, seen in this picture from the *Illustrated Atlas of Will County* (1873), was located between the canal and the railroad. (Courtesy of Gerald W. Adelmann.)

Figure 46. This ca. 1880 view of the I&M Canal in Lockport shows the north end of the Public Landing, along with the Gaylord Building. In 1836 the I&M Canal commissioners created the Public Landing to provide a central open area for commercial traffic (see pl. 49). (Courtesy of Gerald W. Adelmann.)

Figure 47. The large Norton Warehouse, built of local dolomite, occupied the south end of the Public Landing. Across the canal was the Hydraulic Basin, where Norton had a flour-, paper-, and lumber-milling complex (see fig. 45 and pl. 48). (Photograph by Copelin, ca. 1870. Courtesy of Gerald W. Adelmann.)

In the 1890s the use of local dolomite for buildings declined, giving way to a superior gray limestone that was quarried in Bedford, Indiana. Labor strife and the resulting wage increases left Des Plaines River valley quarries unable to compete with the lower prices that nonunionized quarries in Indiana could offer. Perhaps more significant, though, was the quality of the dolomite itself: its softness led to spalling and made it a difficult stone to quarry for building purposes. After the turn of the century, most Lemont, Lockport, and Joliet quarries were used exclusively for gravel and crushed stone.

RAILS AND STEEL

In 1851 Joliet became the first Des Plaines River valley community to have a railroad. By 1855 it had surpassed Lockport in size, marking the relative importance of the railroad to the Illinois and Michigan Canal. Joliet developed rapidly in the nineteenth century as a rail hub and attracted numerous manufacturers, owing to its water and rail access.

In 1869, the same year that the transcontinental railroad was completed, the Joliet works of the Union Coal, Iron, and Transportation Company

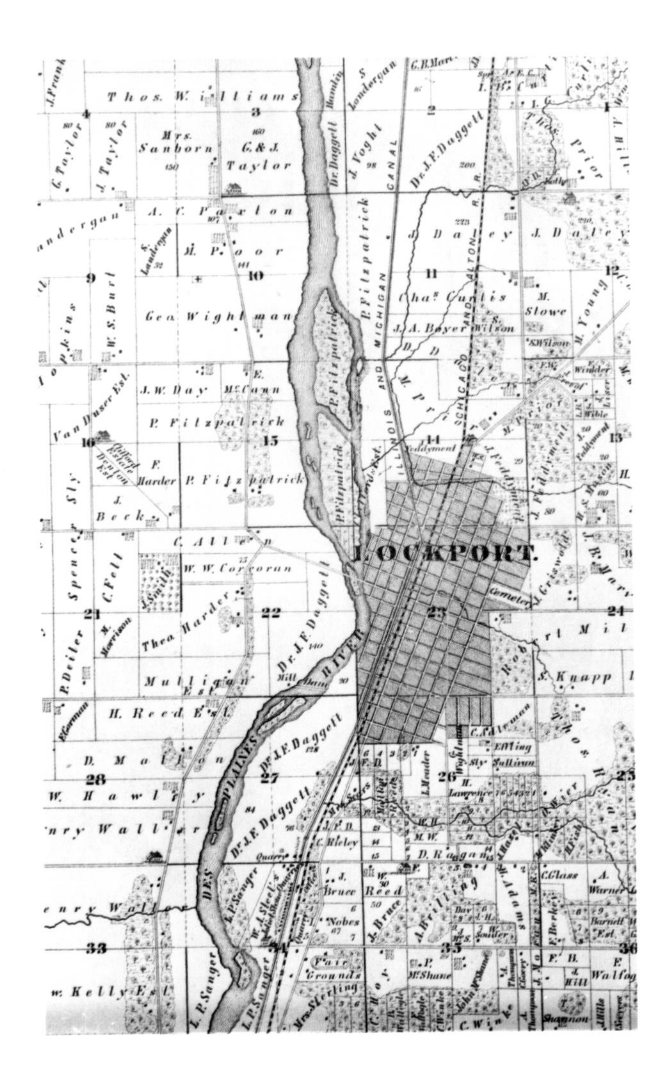

Figure 48. This map of Lockport appeared in the *Illustrated Atlas of Will County* (1873). (Courtesy of Gerald W. Adelmann.)

opened. The plant, which would later be known as Joliet Iron and Steel, then American Steel and Wire, and finally U.S. Steel Corporation, manufactured barbed wire, iron, and eventually steel rails. In 1873 it became one of the first plants in the nation to add Bessemer converters for the production of steel. Like the giant steel plants located along the Cal-Sag Channel, the Joliet plant made good use of the I&M Canal and the Des Plaines River as water and transportation sources, as well as the rail lines that ran through it. Numerous other steel-related manufactures grew up in Joliet, and by the turn of the century steel had replaced stone as the city's dominant industry.

While the steel plant still operates in Joliet (under the ownership of Birmingham Steel Corporation), the blast furnaces were dismantled in the 1930s. The foundations (see pl. 52) will form the heart of an interpretive trail in the new Joliet Iron Works Historic Site. The park itself will be an excellent vantage point for understanding Carl Sandburg's view of Joliet.

Figure 49. Patrick Fitzpatrick, an Irish immigrant, came to Lockport in 1833 as a laborer or small contractor on the I&M Canal. A successful farmer, he eventually amassed 1,200 acres of land (see fig. 48). In 1848 he began construction of this Greek Revival farmhouse made of locally quarried stone. Thanks to a donation by Material Service Corporation, the restored Fitzpatrick House now serves as the headquarters for the Illinois and Michigan Canal National Heritage Corridor.

Figure 50. In the 1890s the Unitarian Universalist Church built this mixed-use structure of local stone on Clinton Street in downtown Joliet to combine commercial and office space with its sanctuary.

Figure 51. This view of the "Joliet Quarries, Hon. W. A. Steel., Prop.," which appeared in the *Illustrated Atlas of Will County* (1873), shows the Chicago, Alton, and St. Louis Railroad in the foreground, the I&M Canal with a boat adjacent to the quarry, and the Des Plaines River in the background. Plate 52 shows one of the present-day remnants of this quarry. (Courtesy of the Newberry Library, Chicago.)

Joliet

On the one hand the steel works.
On the other hand the penitentiary.
Santa Fe trains and Alton trains
Between smokestacks on the west
And grey walls on the east.
And Lockport down the river.
Part of the valley is God's.
And part is man's.

The river course laid out
A thousand years ago.
The canals ten years back.
The sun on two canals and one river
Makes three stripes of silver
Or copper and gold
Or shattered sunflower leaves.
Talons of an iceberg
Scraped out this valley.
Claws of an avalanche loosed here.

VALLEY TOWNS AND LANDSCAPES TODAY

After the Great Depression, as the automobile gained prominence over rail and water transport and as technology changed the organization of community life, residential and commercial patterns changed in the Canal Corridor. The downtowns that had clustered along the canal were slowly abandoned by businesses as development migrated toward the interstate highways. A regional shopping mall located along Interstate 55 shifted Joliet's retailing center away from the downtown area, and strip malls did the same for Lemont and Lockport.

In 1991 a regional Main Street program was initiated in the I&M Canal Corridor to help communities preserve the historic character of their downtowns with federal, state, and regional partners providing technical assistance to local volunteers.

As a result, towns like Lockport and Lemont have created Main Street organizations dedicated to preserving their downtowns' historic character and to revitalizing the economy by serving residents and increasing tourist trade.

In the early 1990s riverboat gaming was made legal in Illinois. Joliet, seeking a catalyst for economic revitalization, secured two riverboats, one in its downtown area and one south of the central city. In the short term the riverboats have been phenomenally successful. Local taxes on them have brought millions of dollars to the city's coffers and enabled massive infrastructure improvements, including riverfront and streetscape enhancements in the downtown area. The boats attract six million patrons each year, more than the 5.5 million who visit the parks, trails, and historical societies throughout the Canal Corridor. The future of this economic boon is unknown, but permanent improvements are being installed that will help to shape the character of twenty-first-century Joliet.

THE NATIONAL HERITAGE CORRIDOR

The Illinois and Michigan Canal officially closed in 1933 when the Illinois Waterway opened. That year the Civilian Conservation Corps began a program of improving the canal as a recreational parkway.

Figure 52. The blast furnaces seen in this ca. 1900 view of the Joliet Iron Works, looking east across the I&M Canal, were dismantled in the 1930s. The foundations survive and will be used in a new interpretive park (see pl. 53). (Photograph by William L. Hurd. Courtesy of Dr. Robert E. Sterling Collection, Joliet, Ill.)

Figure 53. In this ca. 1900 view of Joliet, the I&M Canal runs parallel to the Des Plaines River. The canal was modified when the Sanitary and Ship Canal was built, and portions of it, including Lock No. 5, were removed between 1931 and 1933, when Brandon Lock and Dam was built as part of the Illinois Waterway. (Photograph by William L. Hurd. Courtesy of Dr. Robert E. Sterling Collection, Joliet, Ill.)

Figure 54. Joliet's beautifully restored Jacob Henry Mansion, built in 1873, is listed on the National Register of Historic Places.

Figure 55. The Joliet riverboat gaming pavilion and downtown riverwalk, 1996.

Figure 56. Construction of the Joliet riverboat gaming pavilion and downtown riverwalk, 1993.

The CCC converted miles of towpath into hiking and bicycling trails and rehabilitated locks, sections of the canal, and various structures, such as lock-tenders' houses. But the state government failed to maintain many of these improvements. In the 1950s and 1960s the Adlai E. Stevenson Expressway was constructed along the canal's first seven miles, with other portions of the canal being sold to municipalities such as Lemont. A grassroots response to these actions resulted in the designation of the 61.5-mile Illinois and Michigan Canal State Trail in 1974.

Throughout the 1970s conservation-minded citizens continued to be frustrated at the slow pace of the state's development of the Canal Trail and at the neglect of the eastern reaches of the canal in the Des Plaines River valley. In his front-page

Chicago Tribune series entitled "Our Hidden Wilderness," John Husar wrote, "While other cities fight for breathing room, Chicago has a virtually untapped recreational corridor hidden behind the smokestacks and fences and freight yards in the 25-mile-long Des Plaines River Valley."

In the 1980s citizens who appreciated the historic and natural sites along the I&M Canal joined forces with corporate leaders who recognized the value of enhancing the region's quality of life for their workforce. Conservationists and historic preservationists began to work with municipal, regional, and state leaders who recognized that attracting tourists could provide an economic boost to communities that were losing heavy industry and downtown businesses. The result was legislation creating the first National Heritage Corridor, a concept endorsed by a coalition of business, civic, and conservation interests.

The Illinois and Michigan Canal National Heritage Corridor is intended to link historic sites, canals, and canal towns with parks, trails, and nat-

Figure 57. In a historic agreement between conservationists, business leaders, and local, regional, state, and federal governments, 19,000 acres of the Joliet Army Arsenal were transferred to the U.S. Forest Service in 1996 to become the Midewin National Tallgrass Prairie (see pls. 3 and 59). Fences erected for cattle make the prairie park an ideal place to reintroduce bison to Illinois. The site is part of a 40,000-acre "macro site" encompassing nearby conservation areas such as Goose Lake Prairie that create unparalleled wildlife habitats for numerous native Illinois species.

Figure 58. Goose Lake Prairie, located just west of the Midewin National Tallgrass Prairie, is the largest remaining tract of native tallgrass prairie in Illinois. This aerial view, looking northeast across Goose Lake Prairie State Natural Area to the Illinois River, shows the Dresden Nuclear Power Plant, which came on line in 1960 as the first privately financed nuclear plant in the United States.

ural areas, including prairies, wetlands, and woodlands, in a 450-square-mile area. The national designation brings with it only modest funds, but it has succeeded in changing local and state perceptions of the I&M Canal and the region. Although no federal land ownership or regulation was added by the designation, it has created a framework for conservation, fostering prairie restoration and miles of trails and greenways. Nationally recognized projects, such as the restoration of Lockport's Gaylord

Figure 59. Goose Lake Prairie was named for a glacial lake that once attracted flocks of water fowl during annual migrations. The lake was drained in the late nineteenth century to mine the clay deposits underneath. With leadership from Openlands Project, the Illinois Department of Conservation acquired 1,440 acres of this grassland in 1969, preventing its use for clay mining or industrial development.

Building and the creation of the 19,000-acre Midewin National Tallgrass Prairie, are becoming major regional destination points, while new parks and rehabilitated downtown buildings improve the quality of life for local residents.

In an area dominated by sprawling metropolitan growth, the National Heritage Corridor designation has created a rare regional identity and fostered unprecedented cooperation among units of government, businesses, and citizens. One hundred fifty years after the I&M Canal opened the Midwest to commerce, the citizens of the Canal Corridor have embarked on another long-term public improvement project: a new kind of national park that uses the canal as its centerpiece and celebrates the region's history, preserves its natural landscapes, and contributes to a healthy regional economy.

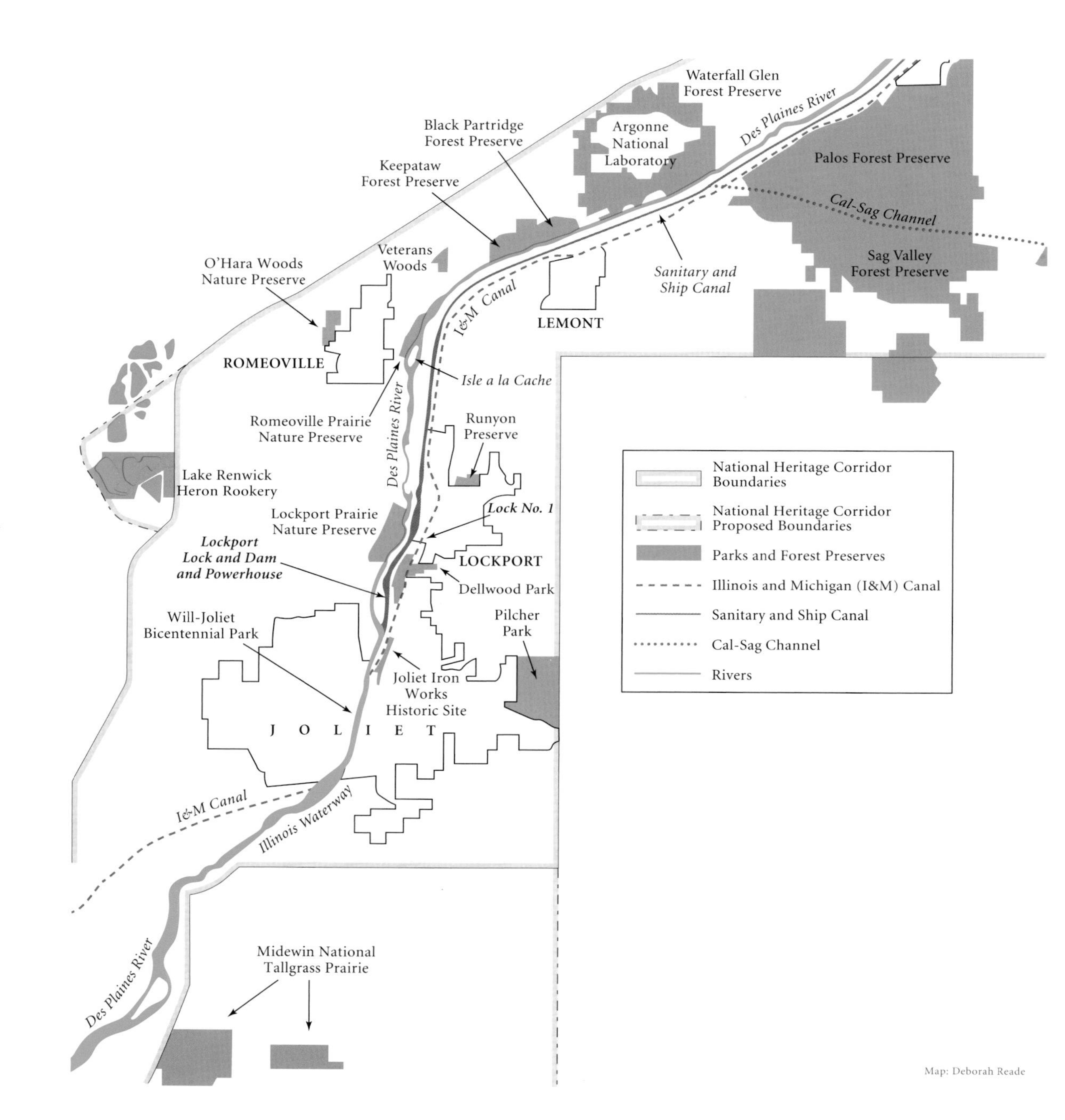

PORTFOLIO PLATES

PLATE 40. The I&M Canal is the snow-lined narrow waterway visible to the left of the Sanitary and Ship Canal. West of Lemont, the Sanitary Canal is used intensively for shipping gravel from nearby quarries. The Des Plaines River is the waterway on the right.

PLATE 41. The Sanitary Canal is still an active industrial waterway in Lemont. The high bridge provides the major entry into Lemont from Interstate 55.

PLATE 42. When the Illinois Department of Transportation began selling off portions of the I&M Canal in the 1960s, the village of Lemont purchased a five-mile segment, intending to fill it with industrial development and parking lots. With the National Heritage Corridor designation came a change of heart, and the village has recently developed a 1.5-mile recreational and interpretive trail. Lemont residents and village leaders now see the canal as the centerpiece of the community's downtown revitalization program.

PLATE 43. These historic buildings, many with false fronts, house antique shops, restaurants, and boutiques, such as the one located in the "Touch of Class" building with its cast-iron façade. The extended façade of the building to the right is set at a different angle, to follow a bend in the street where the grid pattern shifted to follow the railroad tracks behind it.

PLATE 44. This refinery has operated continuously since 1922 under a variety of owners. It is near the former Texaco refinery in Lockport, which opened in 1911 and was the first to bring the petroleum industry to the Canal Corridor. The I&M Canal runs through the refinery.

PLATE 45. Isle a la Cache, where French *voyageurs* hid their trade goods, was acquired in 1983 as an interpretive site by the Forest Preserve District of Will County. Beavers continue to make their home on the island.

PLATE 46. This reconstructed wigwam is used by costumed interpreters who tell stories of Native American culture and the French fur trade to hundreds of schoolchildren from the region.

PLATE 47. The shallow soil of the Des Plaines River valley created an unusual wet dolomite prairie in Lockport. Home to the extremely rare leafy prairie clover, the 259-acre prairie along the banks of the Des Plaines River was threatened by dumping and off-road vehicles. In 1983 local citizens and regional conservation organizations succeeded in preserving the area. It is now an Illinois Nature Preserve, owned by the Metropolitan Water Reclamation District of Greater Chicago and managed and interpreted by the Forest Preserve District of Will County.

PLATE 48. The I&M Canal Public Landing has become a focus for historic preservation in Lockport and the beginning of a two-mile local canal trail. The Norton Warehouse, seen through the trees, has been restored to combine commercial and residential space (see figs. 45 and 47).

PLATE 49. The original one-and-a-half-story portion of this building was adjacent to the I&M Canal and was built in 1838 as a materials and construction equipment depot. The three-story office portion was added in 1859. George Gaylord, a grain merchant and quarry operator, opened a dry goods store in the building in 1878.

One hundred years later, the building, cut off from the downtown area by railroad tracks and adjacent to a canal that was all but abandoned, was altered, vacant, and in danger of collapse. The philanthropist Gaylord Donnelley, a leader in the movement to create a National Heritage Corridor, was intrigued to learn that his grandfather owned the building and agreed to form a private company to restore it, hoping that renovation of the building would spur a larger regional revitalization effort.

In 1986 the restored Gaylord Building received the President's Award for Historic Preservation. In 1996 Mrs. Gaylord Donnelley donated the building to the National Trust for Historic Preservation as its first commercial historic property. The building contains a visitors' center, a gallery of the Illinois State Museum, and a fine restaurant (see fig. 46).

PLATE 50. This was designated the first lock on the I&M Canal, after the two summit-level locks at Bridgeport and Romeoville. The lock was preserved as a result of the Illinois and Michigan Canal National Heritage Corridor designation.

PLATE 51. Starting in 1991, volunteers in Lockport formed a Main Street organization, which is sucessfully promoting revitalization of this intact streetscape. The building of local dolomite shown at the corner housing a hardware store was the only one on the block to survive downtown Lockport's extensive fire in 1895.

PLATE 52. This quarry (see fig. 51) was one of the more than fifty dolomite quarries that produced building stone in the Des Plaines River valley during the nineteenth century. The quarry is within a 176-acre parcel acquired by the Lockport Township Park District, known as Dellwood Park West. The planned ecological park also includes prairie savanna remnants and Native American archaeological sites and is adjacent to three locks on the I&M Canal. It will be linked by a 2.7-mile canal trail to the Joliet Iron Works Historic Site.

PLATE 53. In the 1930s U.S. Steel demolished its six major blast furnaces, leaving only the foundations. In 1989 it was persuaded to donate forty-five acres to the Corporation for Openlands (CorLands), including the foundations of its historic blast furnaces, engine house, and other steel-making structures. These remains are being incorporated into the Joliet Iron Works Historic Site, to be opened by the Forest Preserve District of Will County in 1998.

PLATE 54. This opulent theater, designed by the Chicago-based architects C. W. and George Rapp, opened in 1926 and combined Greek, Roman, and Italian Renaissance styles. In 1974, at a time when movie palaces across the country were being demolished, local citizens mounted a campaign to save the Rialto. In 1978 the Rialto complex was acquired by a new public entity, and in 1981 the restored theater reopened.

PLATE 55. In the 1960s Joliet's earliest commercial district was razed as part of an urban renewal project. Will-Joliet Bicentennial Park was created in 1976 to commemorate the town's early history. In 1992 the commemorative boulders were relocated temporarily to accommodate construction of a riverwalk. A gaming boat is visible between the school buses, on the opposite side of the river.

PLATE 56. Joliet's bascule bridges reflected trends in bridge design in Chicago. The downtown riverboat gaming entry pavilion is outlined in lights beyond the bridge. A hotel is scheduled for construction adjacent to the pavilion, and the city plans to extend its riverwalk south into the area in the foreground of this photograph.

PLATE 57. In 1992 some of downtown Joliet's earliest stone buildings were demolished to make way for parking lots for the riverboat gaming facility. To the west, historic homes are visible on the bluff across the waterway.

PLATE 58. Mobil's refinery south of Joliet is the company's showcase and Midwest headquarters. Mobil values open space around the refinery as a buffer area, similar to the adjoining Joliet Army Arsenal, and supports conservation efforts on its own as well as surrounding lands.

PLATE 59. In the 1960s and 1970s portions of the 35,000-acre arsenal were sold off to industry and used to create the Des Plaines Conservation Area. In 1992, when it was announced that the remaining 23,000 acres would be sold as surplus land, a coalition of business, conservation, and government leaders came together to develop a plan for reusing the arsenal. The Midewin National Tallgrass Prairie now occupies 19,000 acres. A landfill, industrial park, and veterans' cemetery will also be created on the site of the former ammunitions plant.

40. *Sanitary and Ship Canal, west of Lemont.*

41. *Sanitary and Ship Canal at Lemont.*

42. *I&M Canal, looking east from Lemont.*

43. *Downtown Lemont.*

44. *UnoVen Refinery (now Citgo), Lemont.*

45. *Des Plaines River from Isle a la Cache, Romeoville.*

46. *Wigwam at the Isle a la Cache Nature Museum, Romeoville.*

47. Lockport Prairie.

48. *I&M Canal and the Norton Warehouse, looking south from Lockport.*

49. *Gaylord Building, Lockport.*

50. *I&M Canal Lock No. 1, Lockport.*

51. *State Street in Lockport, looking northeast from 10th Street.*

52. *Abandoned quarry south of Lockport.*

53. *Foundations of hot blast stoves, former U.S. Steel Works, Joliet.*

54. *Rialto Square Theater, Joliet.*

55. *Will-Joliet Bicentennial Park, Joliet.*

56. Des Plaines River/Illinois Waterway looking north, with gaming boat, Joliet.

57. *Downtown Joliet demolition site, looking west.*

58. *Mobil Oil Joliet Refinery, looking southeast.*

59. *Ammunitions Plant, Joliet Army Arsenal.*

CHANNAHON TO MARSEILLES

From Towpath to Recreational Trail

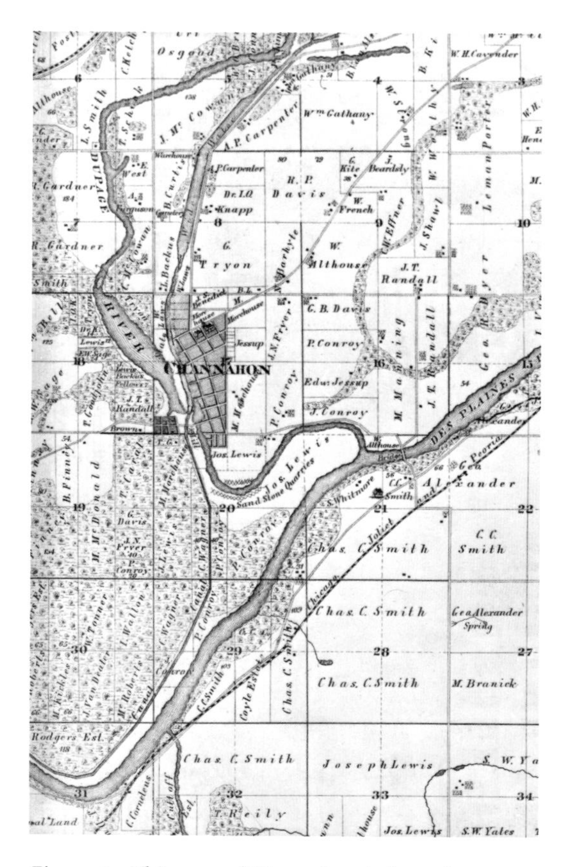

Figure 60. This map of Channahon is from the *Illustrated Atlas of Will County* (1873). (Courtesy of Gerald W. Adelmann.)

Starting at the locktender's house in Channahon (see pl. 62), hikers and bicyclists on the Illinois and Michigan Canal State Trail travel through an agricultural landscape. This rural portion of the Canal Corridor is peaceful and serene, offering an escape from the congestion of the city of Chicago, just thirty-five miles away. Yet the landscape is an engineered one, where waterways have been built, moved, bridged, and dammed, fields have been drained for planting, and stone, coal, and clay have been mined. In the preface to *Nature's Metropolis*, his groundbreaking work on Chicago, William Cronon writes: "Americans have long tended to see city and country as separate places, more isolated from each other than connected. . . . Although we often cross the symbolic boundaries between them – seeking escape or excitement, recreation or renewal – we rarely reflect on how tightly bound together they really are." The I&M Canal provides a striking example of the intimate link between Chicago and its rural hinterland.

In the 1830s the newly invented steel plow enabled settlers to turn over the tough Illinois prairie to produce the nation's richest farmland. When the I&M opened in 1848, farmers gained direct access to Chicago, which quickly became the largest and most efficient grain market in the world. Today, Grundy County, bisected by the canal, still has some of the world's most fertile farmland and is a major producer of corn and beans. Channahon,

Figure 61. This valve control lever at the northeast gate of Lock No. 6 in Channahon was photographed in 1936 by Joseph Hill. (Courtesy of the Historic American Buildings Survey, Library of Congress.)

like nearby Joliet and Lockport, is rapidly losing its farmland to suburban residential developments with access to jobs in Joliet and the western suburbs of Chicago. At the peak of shipping on the I&M, Channahon was dominated by six grain elevators

Figure 62. The Channahon weir crossing the Du Page River, looking toward Lock No. 6 and the locktender's house, ca. 1900. (Courtesy of Dr. Robert E. Sterling Collection, Joliet, Ill.)

around the canal widewater (see fig. 60). Widewaters such as this one were created along the canal to enable boats to stop for storage, loading, and business transactions. When the railroads bypassed Channahon, its canalside commercial center disappeared.

Channahon, meaning "meeting of the waters," is where the Des Plaines and Du Page Rivers converge. The I&M Canal formed yet another confluence in Channahon by crossing the Du Page River at the same water level. Building the ninety-seven-mile canal required a system of locks, dams, aqueducts, culverts, bridges, and weirs to transport boats across streams and rivers and to navigate the 150-foot drop in topography from Bridgeport to La Salle. In Channahon, canal engineers solved the problem of crossing the Du Page by constructing a dam and two locks, one on either side of the river. A weir over the dam allowed mules and horses to pull the canal boats across the Du Page between the locks (see figs. 62–63). A similar system was used to carry canal boats across the Des Plaines River in Joliet.

The I&M's locks were essentially "water elevators" that lifted boats over the change in elevation as the canal descended toward the Mississippi River valley. Locks were 18 feet wide and 110 feet long and generally had a lift of between 5 and 12 feet. During the 1860s, the canal's busiest decade, one locktender reported locking an average of thirty boats a day through the canal (it took about fifteen minutes for a boat to clear a lock). The canal locks were constructed of Joliet and Lemont limestone in the eastern portion and locally quarried sandstone farther west, with hydraulic cement mined and manufactured in Utica used as mortar. Wooden lock gates (now long gone) were attached with iron fittings.

Canal boats were about a hundred feet long and nearly as wide as the locks through which they

Figure 63. This diagram by Tom Willcockson shows the Channahon locks and weir crossing the Du Page River. (From Davis Buisseret's *Historic Illinois from the Air* [Chicago: University of Chicago Press, 1990], 97. © 1990 by The University of Chicago.)

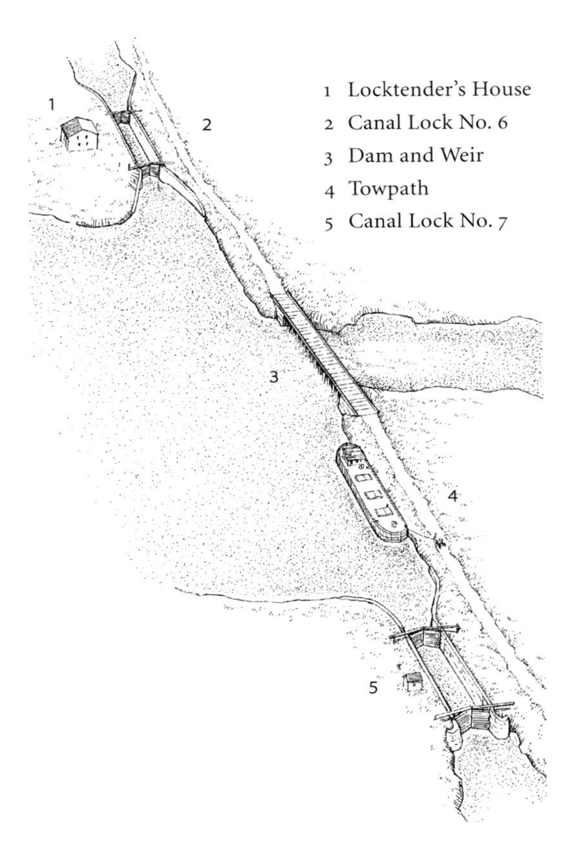

Figure 64. *The Margaret*, a steam-powered canal boat, is shown here approaching Lock No. 6 at Channahon, ca. 1908. This was one of the last boats on the I&M and was used to haul wood from McKinley Woods, near Channahon, to a lime kiln in Joliet. (Courtesy of Dr. Robert E. Sterling Collection, Joliet, Ill.)

Figure 65. The reinforced concrete barrier at the eastern end of Lock No. 7 on the south side of the Du Page River near Channahon was added in 1956, where the wooden lock gates once opened and closed.

had to pass. By 1870 steam-powered boats capable of carrying up to 150 tons of cargo replaced the smaller-capacity, mule-towed barges. Steamboats created wakes that eroded the canal banks, so portions of the canal walls had to be lined with stone. Boatyards along the canal in Chicago, Lockport, and Peru provided repair and construction facilities. In the first year of canal operation 162 boats regularly worked the canal; in later years there were close to 300 boats in active service. The number of boats diminished as their hauling capacities increased. By 1882, when the canal's tonnage exceeded one million, only 32 boats were in service.

Boat designs varied to accommodate different cargoes, including grain, lumber, and stone. Packet boats carrying passengers were used only until the mid-1850s, when railroads replaced the canal for passenger travel. These boats were pulled by horses, which traveled faster than mules. In the few short years that passengers traveled the I&M Canal, millions made the twenty-two- to twenty-six-hour journey from Chicago to La Salle, replacing a minimum thirty-six-hour trip by stagecoach. One packet boat traveler, Sir Arthur Cunynghame, described the crowded conditions in 1851 in his book *A Glimpse at the Great Western Republic:*

The cabin of this canal boat was about 50 feet in length, 9 feet wide, and 7 feet high. We numbered about ninety passengers within this confined space, in which we were to sleep, eat and live; the nominal duration of our passage was twenty hours, but it eventually proved to be twenty-five; our baggage was secured on the roof of the boat, and covered with canvass, to screen it from the effects of the weather; . . . sleeping places consisted of shelves placed three deep, the entire length of the cabin, on either side, with a height of two feet between each.

Figure 66. This early timber structure in the former settlement of Dresden is thought to be the I&M Canal's last surviving mule barn. These barns were maintained about every fifteen miles along the canal route. Teams of two to five mules were attached to the boats by a 150-foot-long line and were led on the towpath by muleskinners, usually boys about fourteen years old. The canal was also populated with boat captains, crew members (boats generally had a total crew of five), locktenders, towpath walkers (checking for damage), toll collectors, and tavern keepers.

The dam and weir built across the Du Page River at Channahon were one solution to transporting canal boats over other bodies of water. Another was to build aqueducts, such as those over Aux Sable Creek and Nettle Creek in Grundy County and the longer Fox River Aqueduct in La Salle County (see figs. 67 and 75–76; see also pls. 70 and 76). For smaller streams a simpler solution consisted of constructing culverts to divert creeks under the canal.

Just outside Channahon the Des Plaines and Kankakee Rivers come together to form the Illinois River. Within the broad Illinois River valley, the towns of Morris, Marseilles, and Seneca evolved as

Figure 67. The Aux Sable Aqueduct, seen in this aerial view along with Lock No. 8, is 136 feet long. The complex of buildings adjacent to the lock includes one of the I&M Canal's two remaining locktender's houses (see pl. 62).

Figure 68. Looking west from Lock No. 8 at Aux Sable.

canal shipping centers. Grain elevators brought farmers from this rich agricultural area to these towns to add their produce into the "golden stream" of international commerce that flowed through Chicago. The Morris and Marseilles skylines were also punctuated by smokestacks of factories and breweries. When the railroads arrived they added spurs to their lines to reach the canalside factories and grain elevators and gave industry new opportunities to build factories throughout the towns. Channahon and Dresden stopped growing when the railroads bypassed them. Morris continues to

Figure 69. A postcard of the I&M Canal and factories in Morris, ca. 1910. (Courtesy of the Morris Public Library.)

Figure 70. A postcard of the grain elevator at Seneca, ca. 1915. (Courtesy of Ruth Packham.)

Figure 71. A railroad bridge crosses the I&M Canal near Gebhard Woods State Park in Morris.

thrive as the county seat of agriculturally prosperous Grundy County.

Illinois means "river of men" or simply "the men" in the language of the Illinois tribe. The Illinois River truly is a river of men – continually traveled and reshaped to meet human needs. During the Upper Mississippian period (A.D. 1200–1500), mounds and village sites lined the river valleys, concentrating at confluence sites like Channahon. The I&M Canal was the first chapter in a quest to create a deep navigable waterway from Lake Michigan to the Mississippi River. The completion of the Sanitary and Ship Canal to Joliet in 1908 created a far more advanced channel and fueled efforts to either expand the I&M or find another solution to create a continuous deep waterway.

Figure 72. The rapids at Marseilles were used for water power beginning in 1832, when the first saw mill was established. The Illinois Waterway Dam at Marseilles, shown in this aerial view looking west, was constructed over the river rapids in 1933 using two diversion dams to fuel industries and a hydroelectric plant. The extensive complex of buildings to the right of the bridge once housed the cardboard box–making factory owned by the National Biscuit Co. (Nabisco), which was the heart of Marseilles's paper-making industry. The bridge spanning the Illinois River, just west of the dam, was constructed in 1932 and is currently being replaced (see pl. 74). The eight fully loaded barges near the bridge are being pushed toward the Marseilles lock 2.5 miles downstream.

In 1921 the state began construction of the Illinois Waterway by channelizing the Des Plaines and Illinois Rivers between the terminus of the Sanitary Canal in Joliet and the Mississippi River. The river was dammed and dredged to a consistent depth of nine feet. Construction was delayed when the state ran out of funds during the Great Depression and was completed by the U.S. Army Corps of Engineers in 1933. The Canal Corridor landscape was once again re-engineered to meet the commercial needs of the nation.

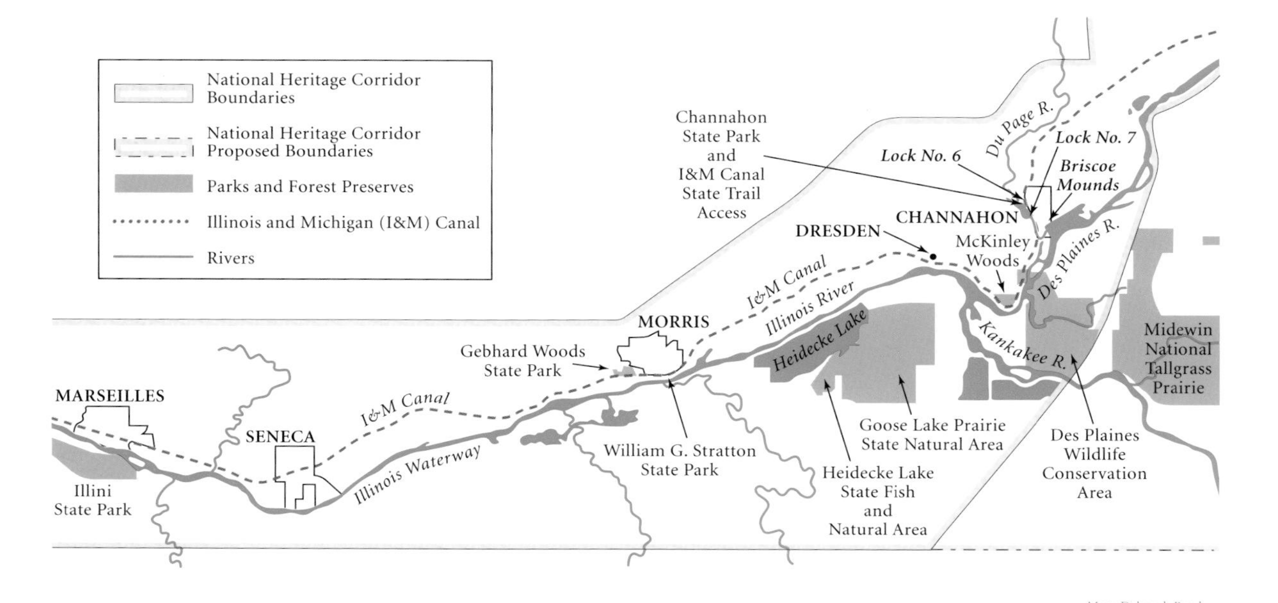

Map: Deborah Reade

PORTFOLIO PLATES

PLATE 60. Archaeological remains point to extensive Native American settlement in the region between Channahon and Morris during the Upper Mississippian period (A.D. 1200–1500). In the 1980s Material Service Corporation donated these two mounds that were associated with a large village site to the Illinois State Museum, protecting them from the quarrying and development that have destroyed many other mound sites in the region.

PLATE 61. Lock No. 6 is visible to the right in this photograph. A weir extended across the slow-moving Du Page River between Lock No. 6 and Lock No. 7 (see figs. 61–63).

PLATE 62. Twelve locktenders' houses once stood along the I&M Canal. This one, and another at Lock No. 8 in Aux Sable (see fig. 67), are the only two in existence today. Both are to be rehabilitated using federal funds.

PLATE 63. The park at Channahon is a popular destination for weekend visitors and an important access point to the I&M Canal State Trail.

PLATE 64. The town of Dresden developed around a stagecoach stop before the canal was built, but it was virtually abandoned after the railroads bypassed it in 1852. The only surviving buildings are this tavern, now used as a farmhouse, seen here across the canal, and a mule barn (see fig. 66).

PLATE 65. The stretch of the trail between Channahon and Marseilles offers beautiful scenery and access to some of the best-preserved portions of the canal. McKinley Woods, owned by the Forest Preserve District of Will County, includes recreational structures built by the Civilian Conservation Corps while improving the canal in the 1930s.

PLATE 66. In 1996 heavy rains washed out the dam at Channahon, causing the twelve-mile scenic stretch of the canal between Channahon and Morris to go dry. The remains of seven canal boats, dating from the 1870s and 1880s, were exposed in the wide-water at Morris, enabling archaeologists to study the boats used on the canal. Too fragile to be removed, the boats will be resubmerged when the canal is again filled with water in 1998.

PLATE 67. A contemporary painting of Chief Shabbona, based on an 1857 ambrotype, can be seen in the display. Shabbona, a Potawatomi chief, spent most of his life in the Canal Corridor. He played an important role in the interaction between European settlers and Native Americans (see pp. 37–39).

PLATE 68. The courthouse lawn contains monuments honoring local war veterans, as well as an Indian ceremonial pole (see fig. 7).

PLATE 69. Once Morris's largest employer, the Coleman Hardware Company was owned by Joseph Coleman, a Chicagoan. The company's extensive complex along the I&M Canal was served by railroad spurs. Today the buildings lie in ruins between the downtown area and Gebhard Woods State Park.

PLATE 70. The aqueduct carrying the canal over Nettle Creek is located within Gebhard Woods State Park. The towpath in Morris is used extensively by local residents for exercise and recreation.

PLATE 71. Some of the highest-grade farming soil in the nation can be found between Morris and Ottawa. Corn has continuously been one of the region's greatest products, and the canal facilitated shipping it and other grains to international markets.

PLATE 72. Petroleum- and chemical-processing industries coexist with agriculture in the Morris area.

PLATE 73. The last surviving nineteenth-century elevator on the I&M Canal, shown here, was also served by a railroad spur. The sixty-five-foot-tall, 70,000-bushel-capacity elevator was built in 1862 by John Armour. Though much smaller than the 850,000-bushel-capacity elevator Armour's brother owned in Chicago, the Seneca elevator reportedly shipped 900,000 bushels of grain in 1876. In the 1890s as many as 400 wagons patronized the elevator in a single day. The elevator closed in the 1940s and will be rehabilitated by the state of Illinois as an interpretive site. (see fig. 70)

PLATE 74. This bridge replaced a 1932 steel bridge (see fig. 72).

60. *Briscoe Burial Mound, near Channahon.*

61. *Confluence of the Du Page River and the I&M Canal at Lock No. 6, Channahon.*

62. *Lock No. 6 and the locktender's house, Channahon.*

63. Channahon State Park and the Du Page River, from I&M Canal State Trail bridge abutments, Channahon.

64. *I&M Canal and the Rutherford Tavern, Dresden.*

65. I&M Canal State Trail, near McKinley Woods Forest Preserve.

66. *Canal boat remains, I&M Canal, Morris.*

67. Morris Fire Station display window.

68. *Vietnam Veterans Memorial, Morris.*

69. *Smokestack, Coleman Hardware Building, seen from the I&M Canal State Trail, Morris.*

70. *Nettle Creek Aqueduct, I&M Canal, Morris.*

71. *Cornfield, Morris area.*

72. *Enron Petroleum works, near Morris.*

73. *Seneca Grain Elevator.*

74. *Bridge construction on the Illinois River at Marseilles in 1996, looking east.*

OTTAWA TO LA SALLE/PERU

Cultures Converge

At Ottawa, the Fox River flows into the Illinois River and the Illinois River valley noticeably deepens and widens. A souvenir publication by E. A. Nattinger describes the valley's scenery as both "savage" and "softly beautiful":

The bluffs, which at Ottawa are 85 feet high, at Utica extend 100 feet in altitude and to the west are still higher – 150 feet. The bluffs are vast, often vertical walls of St. Peter's sandstone, a soft rock easily acted upon by water, heat and cold. . . . The consequence is that these rocky walls present a continuous succession of over-hanging cliffs, gorges of projecting masses, much resembling the ruins of some gigantic and massive structure.

Today this part of the canal region is best known for its natural beauty, parks, and trails. Millions flock to Starved Rock State Park to hike through its canyons, fish in the Illinois River, and watch the eagles, heron, and osprey. The Fox River, just north of Ottawa, with its scenic sandstone bluffs, is the most popular canoe route in the state. The I&M Canal State Trail, Buffalo Rock and Matthiessen State Parks, and the W. D. Boyce Memorial Boy Scout Trail also attract visitors and offer respite to local residents.

The western segment of the Canal Corridor features the greatest concentration of Native American remains. The region's landmarks include sites of the first contact between Europeans and Indians in the 1670s. By 1800 the tribes that inhabited the area were gone, and in the 1830s canal construction created a new impetus for settlement. The same geology that created the region's scenic bluffs and canyons supplied mineral riches for coal-, sand-, and cement-mining industries, which expanded the towns in the nineteenth century.

Ottawa, Utica, La Salle, and Peru boomed in the 1830s, when Irish canal workers joined Yankee settlers from New England. Ottawa and La Salle were platted by the canal commissioners; Utica and Peru were privately developed to take advantage of the transportation route as well as the mineral and industrial resources of the area. Canal workers erected many typically Irish houses along the north valley bluffs and the river bottoms, built with sod

walls and thatched roofs. In 1836 tensions over living and working conditions led to the brief but violent riots known as the Irish Rebellion. A posse of sheriffs from Ottawa and Peru joined forces to stop a destructive mob of Irish workers, opening fire on them and leaving a dozen dead and sixty in the Ottawa jail.

Between 1848 and 1860 Germans fleeing political upheavals were the primary immigrants to the area. Later immigrants included Italians who came to the area around 1900 to work in local sand and coal mines and in the glass factories.

OTTAWA

Ottawa was named for one of the last Indian tribes to dominate northern Illinois. The town was originally conceived as the terminus of the Illinois and

Figure 73. Although construction of the Illinois Waterway in 1933 channelized the Illinois River, its islands and meandering shape reflect its original character. The aqueduct that carried the I&M Canal over the Fox River is visible in the lower right corner of this aerial view, looking southwest from Ottawa. The town of Ottawa developed on both sides of the confluence of the Fox and Illinois Rivers, with its downtown clustered a block from the waterfront near the bridge that crosses the Illinois River.

Figure 74. In this detail from an 1895 balloon view of Ottawa, drawn and published by C. J. Paul, Milwaukee, Wis., the I&M Canal is seen crossing the Fox River in the upper right corner. The Lateral Canal, which is perpendicular to the I&M and appears in the center of the image, extended south a half-mile and then turned east, back toward the Fox River at the edge of downtown Ottawa. The east-west segment parallel to the Illinois River was known as the Hydraulic Basin and was connected to the Fox River by a mill race that dropped approximately thirty feet. Additional mill races powered various industries and were located on either side of the lock connecting the I&M to the Lateral Canal. (Courtesy of Edmund Thornton.)

Michigan Canal and was platted by the canal commissioners as a bookend–sister city to Chicago. It became the La Salle County seat, and though engineering considerations eventually made its rival town, La Salle, the canal terminus, Ottawa's advantages over La Salle included the Lateral Canal built in 1839 to afford water power and easy access to the canal and its diverse manufacturing economy.

The Lateral Canal was nearly fifty feet wide through the town and was lined on either side with flour mills, grain elevators, and furniture and hardware manufacturers. By the 1880s the attached Hydraulic Basin was used by eight industries for powering machinery, including a starch factory, a brick- and tile-manufacturing plant, a box factory, and several flour mills.

The Lateral Canal and Hydraulic Basin were filled in and paved over in 1932, just before the I&M Canal officially closed. Runoff from strip mines later filled the I&M on Ottawa's outskirts,

Figure 75. The Fox River Aqueduct, ca. 1900–1920 (see pl. 76). (Courtesy of Ruth Packham.)

Figure 76. The Fox River Aqueduct pier undergoing restoration in 1996.

and concern about flooding caused town leaders to fill the canal in town as well. Although the canal is now dry, one of its most interesting engineering features, the Fox River Aqueduct, survives in Ottawa. Federal funds are being used to restore its deteriorated Joliet limestone piers. The aqueduct's steel trough, supported by seven piers, remains a testament to the engineering challenges faced by builders of the I&M. The last surviving tollhouse on the canal is also in Ottawa (see fig. 4).

In 1991 Ottawa joined the Main Street revitalization program and quickly made re-enactment of the famous 1858 debate over slavery between Abraham Lincoln and Stephen A. Douglas a top priority. The first re-enactment, staged in 1992, attracted hundreds to downtown Ottawa, and in 1993 the event was televised nationally. The original debate, the first in a series around the state, had brought nearly ten thousand people to Ottawa's Washington Square (see pl. 78). According to a contemporary account: "Ottawa was deluged in dust. By wagon, by rail, by canal, the people poured in, till Ottawa was one mass of active life. Men, women, and children, old and young, the dwellers on the broad prairies, had turned their backs upon the plough, and had come to listen to these champions

Figure 77. A La Salle street scene, ca. 1915, photographed by Fr. Dominic Brugger. (Courtesy of St. Bede's Academy, Peru.)

Figure 78. Grain elevators lined the Lateral Canal in Ottawa, seen in this ca. 1870 stereograph by W. E. Bowman, including those owned by the abolitionist John Hossack and his family from 1860 to 1880. (Courtesy of James Jensen.)

of the two parties. Military companies were out; martial music sounded, and salutes of artillery thundered in the air."

Because the industrial policy of Whigs like Lincoln subsidized the construction of canals and railroads, towns like Ottawa and Chicago boomed. Lincoln was no stranger to Ottawa or the canal. In 1852 he was appointed a commissioner to hear claims against the state for damages to property resulting from the construction of the I&M. He spent several days in Ottawa before reconvening the hearings in Chicago and Springfield.

In 1858, when Lincoln debated Douglas in Washington Square, the local audience was receptive to his ideas. He was cheered when he said, "There is no reason in the world why the Negro is not entitled to all the natural rights enumerated in the Declaration of Independence." The most prominent of several Ottawa stops on the Underground Railroad was the home of John Hossack, a canal contractor and grain elevator owner (see fig. 78). In 1859 Hossack and other residents defied federal law to rescue a fugitive slave from the U.S. marshal in Ottawa. Hossack was tried in federal court in Chicago and found guilty but was sentenced to only a nominal term because of the city's sympathetic political climate.

While the Lincoln-Douglas debate was clearly Ottawa's most famous downtown event, the city's center generally remained a busy gathering place

in the nineteenth and early twentieth centuries. In addition to serving as a retailing, shipping, and industrial center, Ottawa was a focus of judicial activity. The La Salle County Courthouse, the Appellate Court, and for a time a branch of the Illinois State Supreme Court brought lawyers to live and work in Ottawa. By 1870 there were eleven hotels in town. Ottawa's scenery and educated community made it attractive to Chicagoans, including Marshall Field, who had a summer residence there, and W. D. Boyce, the founder of the Boy Scouts, who moved to Ottawa in 1903.

Now, a century later, though downtown Ottawa is no longer a center for lodging, it continues to boast a service industry centered around the courthouse and banks – and, increasingly, around tourists. While many of the community's retail establishments have moved to the fringes of town or to Peru's regional mall, downtown Ottawa is receiving new life because of the banks and government agencies that have renewed their commitment to staying in the central area, the entrepreneurs who are rehabilitating Ottawa's historic brick buildings, and the volunteers working to revitalize the center of the city through the Main Street program.

A PASSAGEWAY FOR THOUSANDS OF YEARS

The Canal Corridor's most significant Native American sites are on the outskirts of Ottawa. Evidence of Native Americans in the area extends back approximately twelve thousand years. Trading linked the Illinois Valley to the civilization centered in Cahokia in the greater St. Louis area. Seashells from Florida found at mounds in Utica, dating from the start of the Christian era, indicate the complexity of Indian trading routes. In 1673 the explorer Louis Jolliet and Fr. Jacques Marquette encountered

Figure 79 (*facing page, top right*). W. E. Bowman's art gallery is visible in the center of his photograph "Instantaneous View, Wirewalking from Bowman's Gallery to Courthouse," taken in downtown Ottawa ca. 1870. (Courtesy of James Jensen.)

Figure 80 (*facing page, bottom right*). This view from the Illinois River bridge looking east is by W. E. Bowman, part of the stereograph series "Souvenirs of the Great Flood, Ice, Ruins, etc.," February 1883. (Courtesy of James Jensen.)

Figure 81. Union Bank, a supporter of Main Street Ottawa, elected to rehabilitate its classical downtown building rather than move away from the city center. The structure burned during renovation, but the bank decided to preserve the character of downtown by rehabilitating the façade.

Figure 82. The county government made a commitment to downtown Ottawa by rehabilitating its 1881 stone courthouse.

Figure 83. Outside Ottawa the valley is lined with bluffs of St. Peter's sandstone that made the area a rich source of silica sand. The sand-mining and glass-making industries developed immediately after the Civil War. One major silica sand quarry is still operated in Ottawa by U.S. Silica, and Libbey Owens Ford continues to manufacture plate glass in the area.

seventy-four partly buried earthen cabins at Kaskaskia, also known as the "Grand Village of the Illinois," less than five miles southwest of present-day Ottawa. The Illinois Indians living at this site farmed corn, beans, and squash. In the summer and early winter they left the village and traveled many miles to hunt bison and elk. These were the Indians, familiar for generations with the trade routes from the Mississippi to the Great Lakes, who showed Jolliet and Marquette the Chicago Portage.

Two years after his first visit to Kaskaskia, Marquette returned to found a mission there, as he had promised. Accounts, retold by the writers of Illinois's WPA history, summon up the encounter of cultures. On his return to Kaskaskia, Marquette "called together a great council. . . . Mats and bear-skins covered the council ground, and four large pictures of the Virgin Mary were hung by pieces of taffeta from lines that had been stretched over-head. The father stood in the center and seated in a circle about him were the 500 chiefs and elders; in the background stood the young men, who numbered about 1,000 in all, and the women and children." An Easter Mass said in the village a few days later would be Marquette's last, as he died on his way back to the French base on Mackinac Island.

Marquette was succeeded by other priests who evangelized to the Indians in a climate of hostility among tribes that intensified when Iroquois raiding parties entered the area. In 1682 Robert Sieur Cavalier de La Salle, attempting to create a gigantic fur-trading empire, constructed Fort St. Louis on top of Starved Rock (then known only as "the Rock" or "Le Rocher") across the Illinois River from Kaskaskia to induce the Illinois Indians to remain in the village after an Iroquois raid. By that time the village had grown dramatically. Archaeologists estimate that in the 1680s the population of the Illinois Valley reached ten thousand.

Figure 84. Kaskaskia, or the "Grand Village of the Illinois" (a.k.a. the Zimmerman Site), where Louis Jolliet and Jacques Marquette encountered thousands of Illinois Indians, was saved from becoming a riverfront housing development in the 1980s by a coalition of activists and state officials.

The French abandoned Fort St. Louis in 1691, and in approximately 1700 the Indians and missionaries moved the entire Kaskaskia village south, to be closer to the main French settlements in the Mississippi River valley near St. Louis. Thereafter the Illinois Valley served as a temporary home and hunting grounds for various Indian tribes during a period of tremendous instability. The Illinois, allied with the French, were almost constantly at war with other tribes, fighting off the Iroquois, Fox, Sac, Potawatomi, Kickapoo, and Ottawa.

According to the legend of Starved Rock, in 1769 the Illinois tribe was under attack. A band of nearly twelve hundred Illinois took refuge on top of the Rock. The tribes fighting the Illinois stronghold realized that attack was futile and decided to

Figure 85. Karl Bodmer's *Wakusásse, Fox Man* (painted ca. 1833) depicts a proud member of one of the major tribes in the Canal Corridor in the turbulent period of the 1670s and 1680s. (Courtesy of the Joslyn Art Museum, Omaha, Nebraska.)

Figure 86. A view of Starved Rock, from W. E. Bowman's series of stereographs "Gems of the Illinois Valley," ca. 1870. (Courtesy of James Jensen.)

Figure 87 (*left*). Split Rock, between Utica and La Salle, is an ancient exposure of St. Peter's sandstone that was cut in half during construction of the I&M Canal and later to accommodate the railroad. The tracks are visible on the left of this D. W. S. Rawson stereograph (1866). (Courtesy of James Jensen.) Figure 88 (*above*). The Illinois River and Starved Rock Lock and Dam are seen in this photograph, looking northeast from Starved Rock toward the area where the "Grand Village of the Illinois" was located. "Lover's Leap," a rocky outcropping that is part of the state park, is on the right.

starve the Illinois into surrender. The Illinois tried to lower buckets to the river for water, but their enemies below cut the lines. Ultimately some starved, others jumped to their deaths, and those who tried to escape were slaughtered. The Rock was henceforth known as "Starved Rock."

The legend of Starved Rock and its scenic vantage point have made it an important destination since the area was settled. Sir Arthur Cunynghame, traveling the I&M Canal in 1850, took a side trip to the rock and reported in *A Glimpse at the Great Western Republic* that "bushels of arrowheads may,

Figure 89. This ca. 1915 photograph by Fr. Dominic Brugger of the I&M Canal and the railroad east of La Salle shows Lock No. 13, now removed, in the background. On the right, a slough between the canal and the Illinois River is flooded by melting snows. (Courtesy of St. Bede's Academy, Peru.)

to this day, be collected on every part of the summit of the rock." As the region developed, Starved Rock became a gathering place and a tourist attraction; it also once housed a private hotel. The rock and surrounding St. Peter's sandstone canyons were acquired as an early Illinois state park in 1911. Today the park and a lodge built by the Civilian Conservation Corps in the 1930s attract over two million visitors annually.

MINERAL RICHES

Marquette and Jolliet also noted the presence of coal in the area, a vestige of ancient forests that

Figure 90. The lime kilns at the Blackball Mines.

Figure 91. The German-American Cement Company of La Salle, depicted in this 1906 photograph by Fr. Dominic Brugger, opened in 1900 on the east bank of the Little Vermilion River along the I&M Canal. In 1919, in response to anti-German sentiment fostered by World War I, the firm changed its name to the La Salle Portland Cement Works. The factory closed in 1970 and reopened as the Illinois Cement Company in 1974 (see the large plant visible just west of the Illinois Central Railroad bridge in fig. 93). (Courtesy of St. Bede's Academy, Peru.)

would secure industrial growth in the towns of La Salle and Peru. Cunynghame, in his 1850 trip, reported on coal pits near the canal. The first mine shaft was sunk in 1856 in La Salle. Later, in 1883, the La Salle/Peru coal industry, which would grow to include nearly fifteen hundred workers, suffered a major labor strike in which primarily immigrant workers successfully fought a wage reduction. Shaft mining gave way to strip mining, which diminished after the World War II era because of competition from other regions with higher-quality and more easily accessible coal.

Coal made the canal terminus area attractive to industry. In 1869 two German entrepreneurs

Figure 92. The aqueduct that carried the I&M Canal over the Little Vermilion River near La Salle is visible in front of the Illinois Central Railroad bridge in this image from D. W. S. Rawson's *The Valley of the Illinois* (1866). The horse-drawn wagon to the right of the aqueduct served as the photographer's portable darkroom. Approximately 450 men were employed in building the massive bridge – a project that was not without the kind of labor controversy typical of the period: after the contractor was killed and 60 workers were arrested, construction proceeded under heavy guard. (Courtesy of the Library of Congress.)

chose to locate their zinc works in La Salle because they needed two tons of coal to smelt each ton of zinc. By the turn of the century the Matthiessen and Hegeler Zinc Works was the nation's largest smelter. Matthiessen, a noted philanthropist and La Salle mayor for nine years, also acquired the Western Clock Company in Peru, the largest manufacturer of alarm clocks in the United States, under the name Westclox. Hegeler founded the philosophical publishing house Open Court Press, which under the leadership of its editor, Paul Carus, became internationally known for establishing connections between Western and Eastern thought (see pls. 89–90).

Limestone, easily made into cement, was discovered in 1837 in the Utica area by canal workers. The Utica Hydraulic Cement Company was founded to supply cement for canal lock construction. The Blackball Mines (see fig. 90) are now an archaeological artifact of this era of cement mining. First opened in the 1870s, the extensive mine included numerous processing structures and a small company town. Today the mines are home to the endangered Indiana bat as well as other species.

THE TRANSPORTATION CORRIDOR

As a center for investment, according to Cunynghame, La Salle had a number of "peculiar advantages":

[I]ts situation at the head of the navigation of the Illinois River, and the termination of the canal, alone would give it consequence, as the place of transshipment of a vast amount of produce from the interior towards the lakes, and of timber from the well-wooded pine forests of Lake Michigan . . . but it has lately been chosen as the spot where three great railroads are to concentrate. . . . There is possibly, therefore, no town in the west where a capitalist could invest with a better chance of a favorable result, than at La Salle.

In 1835 the Illinois Legislature authorized creation of the Illinois Central Railroad (another project supported by Lincoln) from the mouth of the Ohio River to the terminus of the I&M Canal,

Figure 93. The I&M Canal, to the left of the Illinois River in this aerial view looking east from La Salle, broadens into a widewater just past the Little Vermilion Aqueduct and the Illinois Central Railroad bridge. Lock No. 14, with its restored gates, is clearly visible at the bottom of the photograph, just before the canal boat basin. Originally this area also included Lock No. 15, the locktender's house, and the terminal mule barn, where a hundred mules were stabled (see pl. 91).

Figure 94. A riverboat at the I&M Canal turning basin just south of Lock No. 14, ca. 1880. (Courtesy of the La Salle State Bank.)

Figure 95. A fleet of 102 canal barges wait in the La Salle Basin for the opening of navigation, April 9, 1865. (Courtesy of the Illinois State Historical Library.)

but construction of the railroad line was not completed until the 1850s. La Salle was chosen as the site where the railroad would cross the Illinois River on a 2,900-foot-long bridge that was heralded as an engineering wonder. This bridge, crucial to the development of the state, was completed in 1854; in 1893 it was rebuilt on top of its original piers. The reconstruction was organized section by section so as not to interrupt railroad traffic.

The I&M Canal terminated just past the Illinois Central Railroad bridge in La Salle. A widewater area between Lock No. 14 (now restored) and Lock No. 15 created a canal boat basin 640 feet long by 290 feet wide. West of Lock No. 15 was a steamboat basin for river traffic, some 118 feet wide and nearly a mile long (see fig. 93). As the site of the intersection of the canal and the river, La Salle was a busy place, particularly in April, when the canal

Figure 96. As suggested by the parade of grain-carrying wagons in this D. W. S. Rawson image from *The Valley of the Illinois* (1866), Water Street in Peru was a thriving business district. The town's businesses later moved up the bluff to escape not only the congestion associated with railroad traffic but also flooding from the river. Only three of the original buildings in this row survive. (Courtesy of the Library of Congress.)

Figure 97. This scene on Water Street in Peru was typical of what occurred when the Illinois River rose thirty-one feet on January 22, 1916, forcing water and gas plants to close and factories to shut down all the way from Chicago to Peoria. (Courtesy of Maze Lumber.)

was reopened to navigation after being closed all winter. The town evolved a bustling entertainment and hotel industry. Theaters, an opera house, restaurants, hotels, and taverns kept the downtown area strong even after the decline of the canal. During prohibition La Salle's many gambling establishments and stills gave it the name "Little Reno." Even the Blackball Mines were used for illicit brewing and distilling operations (see fig. 90).

While La Salle evolved as a canal town, Peru was a river town. Peru originally developed as the head of navigation on the Illinois River and as a stagecoach terminus from Chicago before the canal was completed. By the 1880s it had two rail lines adjacent to the river along Water Street. The center of the business district along the riverfront was soon crowded by the rails and troubled by perennial flooding. As a result, entrepreneurs moved the downtown away from the water, situating the new commercial center on the high bluffs overlooking the river.

Peru thrived as a locus of the ice-harvesting industry until mechanical refrigeration was introduced in 1890. The local shipyard produced barges that were used to carry Illinois River ice to the cities of the South. At the industry's peak in the 1870s, Peru's sixty-five barges, each loaded with 600–3,500 tons of ice, traveled the Mississippi, Tennessee, Arkansas, and Red Rivers. In the winter ice was harvested from the river and the canal and

Figure 98. Ice fisherman at the terminus of the I&M Canal in La Salle.

loaded directly onto the barges, which were stored frozen in the slough adjacent to the river, with surplus ice stored in icehouses along the canal.

Peru saw its fortunes improve (compared to La Salle) in the mid-twentieth century when highway construction and a high bridge over the river enabled Peru to attract a regional shopping mall as well as other service businesses. Today the twin communities, as well as Utica and Ottawa, struggle to maintain their identities in the face of sprawling growth.

The four towns along the fifteen-mile stretch of the I&M Canal between the Fox River and the canal terminus increasingly recognize that building on their past is the key to surviving into the future. The National Heritage Corridor designation has

Figure 99. High spring floodwaters have submerged the remains of I&M Canal Lock No. 15 in this view from below Lock No. 14 looking west along the channel leading to the Illinois River. The stone pylons were once part of a Chicago, Burlington and Quincy Railroad bridge at Lock No. 15.

generated new interest in the region's multilayered history and brought technical assistance to communities seeking to capture the tourism dollars that visitors to nearby parks represent. Public agencies are following the lead of volunteers and are rehabilitating the canal's locks and aqueducts and enhancing waterfront parks and trails. The designation has also fostered new regional conservation coalitions, like the one formed to save the Kaskaskia Village archaeological site from development. Now owned by the state, the site where Jolliet and Marquette encountered the Illinois Indians 325 years ago will someday become an interpretive park. As citizens plan for the future they are rediscovering the legacies that give the Illinois River valley its special sense of place: the 150-year-old canal, the prehistoric cultures that lived there, the immigrants who settled the region, and the natural resources that define its landscape.

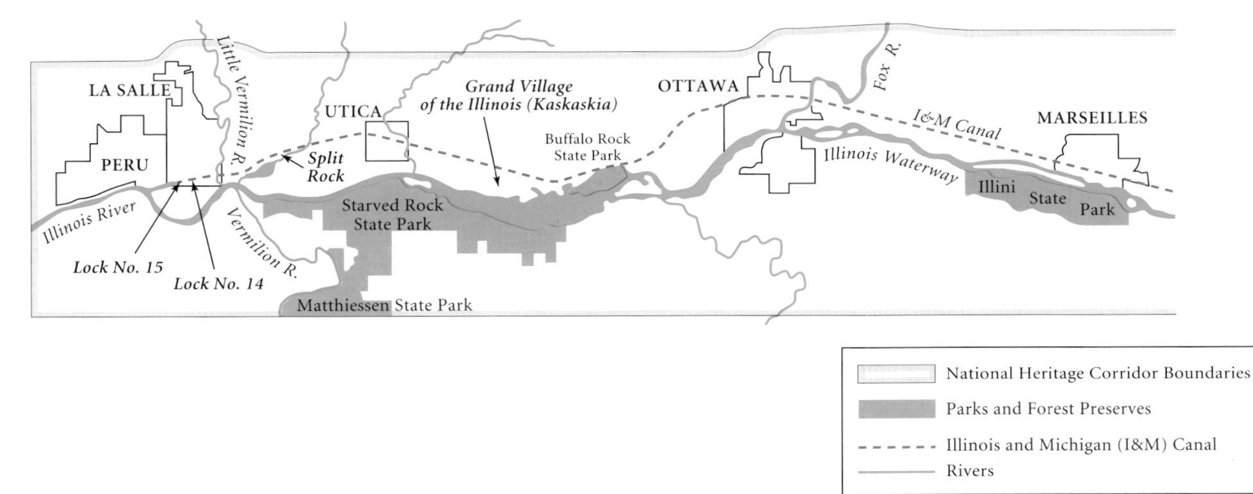

Map: Deborah Reade

PORTFOLIO PLATES

PLATE 75. River traffic continues on the Illinois Waterway.

PLATE 76. In recent years the 464-foot aqueduct was threatened by severe deterioration of its stone piers. A federal grant has allowed the state to begin restoring the piers to match the original design (see figs. 75–76).

PLATE 77. Ottawa's Main Street program is fostering revitalization of its downtown commercial district. The I&M Canal Hydraulic Basin originally ran behind the buildings on the right before it joined the Fox River.

PLATE 78. A glacial boulder was placed in Washington Square to commemorate the site of the 1858 Lincoln-Douglas debate. The 1858 Italianate Reddick Mansion, in the background, now houses civic offices. The steeple of St. Columba Catholic Church, erected in 1882, is visible behind the mansion.

PLATE 79. Ottawa was staunch in its support of the Union and the abolition movement. The names of local soldiers who died are still legible on this limestone monument.

PLATE 80. The canyons and bluffs overlooking the Illinois River once provided campsites for Native Americans. Starved Rock became an early Illinois state park in 1911. Today it is the most visited park in the National Heritage Corridor, with over two million visitors annually to its campgrounds, WPA lodge, and hiking trails.

PLATE 81. The land at the Illinois River bottom is filled with unexplored Native American sites, such as this flagged excavation site near Utica. Archaeologists estimate that ten thousand Indians lived in the area in the 1680s, and evidence points to people having passed through the region as much as twelve thousand years ago.

PLATE 82. Fr. Jacques Marquette, revered for three centuries for his missionary zeal and his knowledge of the New World and its native cultures, made his last voyage through the Prairie Passage. In 1673 he wrote in his journal: "We have seen nothing like this river that we enter, as regards its fertility of soil, its prairies and woods; its cattle, elk, deer, wildcats, bustards, swans, parroquets, and even beaver. There are many small lakes and rivers. That on which we sailed is wide, deep and still." This memorial was dedicated on October 14, 1951. A bronze plaque installed on the Vermont granite base was cast in France from the same mold that was used for a memorial in Marquette's hometown of Laon, France.

PLATE 83. Originally called Science, the town of Utica developed on the banks of the Illinois River but was relocated to the banks of the I&M Canal, where it was platted in 1867. To this day it is a center of gravel and sand mining. Utica's first industry was hydraulic cement mining. The town serves as a gateway for visitors to Starved Rock State Park.

PLATE 84. This grain elevator, erected by the Utica Elevator Company in about 1958, is the last of eight elevators built in the town.

PLATE 85. The I&M Canal State Trail is seen here along the towpath to the left of the frozen canal and just west of the grain elevator in plate 84.

PLATE 86. Constant maintenance is required to keep the canal free of overgrowth, which is particularly dense in areas where the water flow has been reduced.

PLATE 87. The section of the I&M Canal State Trail between Utica and La Salle is one of the most scenic of the 61.5-mile hiking and bicycle trail.

PLATE 88. The canal is used extensively for winter sports, including skating. The Canal Trail is also a favorite of cross-country skiers and snowmobilers.

PLATE 89. This grand second-empire house, designed by the Chicago architect W. W. Boyington (known for Chicago's Water Tower, the Joliet Penitentiary, and other landmarks), contains its original interior finishes. The first floor of the 16,000-square-foot mansion served as the editorial headquarters of Open Court Press from 1895 to 1919.

In 1897 Open Court's publisher brought one of the great Zen scholars, D. T. Suzuki, to work in the mansion for eleven years to translate major Buddhist texts into English. The Carus family recently created the Hegeler Carus Foundation to restore the mansion as a center of philosophical, scientific, and religious dialogue. The family still owns Open Court Press, now best known for publishing *Ladybug, Spider,* and *Cricket* magazines for children.

PLATE 90. Potassium permanganate, used for treating wastewater and for purifying drinking water, is manufactured at this plant, which is located on the site of the former Matthiessen and Hegeler Zinc Works. The transition from mining to chemical processing is consistent with the twentieth-century transformation of industries throughout the Canal Corridor.

PLATE 91. This lock has the only restored gates on the I&M Canal today. A canal boat turning basin was created between Locks No. 14 and 15 in La Salle. The stone walls beyond the lock gates mark the location of Lock No. 15. Beyond Lock No. 15 was a riverboat basin that served as a gateway to the Illinois River (see figs. 93–95).

PLATE 92. The dream of a continuous deep waterway for barge traffic on the Illinois River was realized when the U.S. Army Corps of Engineers built the Illinois Waterway in 1933. Peru has gained prominence over La Salle in the twentieth century because of the commercial activity generated by the automobile bridge over the Illinois River, shown here.

PLATE 93. The waterfront area is no longer a commercial center but continues to house industries and is lined by railroad tracks. The broad Illinois River has become a focal point for state conservation efforts, as erosion problems and flooding continue to challenge navigation and as officials increasingly recognize the value of the natural habitats that line the waterway.

75. Illinois River at its confluence with the Fox River, looking east.

76. Fox River Aqueduct, Ottawa.

77. Downtown Ottawa, looking southeast to the Illinois River from the courthouse.

78. Washington Square, looking north to the Reddick Mansion.

79. *Ottawa Civil War Monument, Washington Square.*

80. *Ottawa Canyon, Starved Rock State Park.*

81. *Archaeological site near Utica.*

82. *Pere Marquette Memorial, Utica.*

83. *Downtown Utica.*

84. *I&M Canal with grain elevator, Utica.*

85. *I&M Canal at Utica, looking west.*

86. *I&M Canal at Utica.*

87. I&M Canal, west of Utica.

88. *Skaters on the I&M Canal at La Salle.*

89. *Hegeler Carus Mansion, La Salle.*

90. *Carus Chemical Corporation, La Salle.*

91. *Lock No. 14, La Salle.*

92. *Illinois River at Peru.*

93. *Illinois River, Peru waterfront.*

94. I&M Canal Lock No. 12, west of Ottawa.

EPILOGUE:
A Love of Stone

WILLIAM LEAST HEAT-MOON

The older I grow the more I believe that our junket through life is one of discovering and acting upon the predilections and passions of some of our ancestors. What certain of them did, we tend to do; what they were, we tend to become. Their inclinations and endeavors and unexplained urgings come around, often slowly, to shape us in ways that we can at first imagine, in the necessarily limited view of our ancestry, to be our very own. After five and some decades of traipsing through my days and wandering around this country and poking into such ancestors' lives as I've been able to uncover, I lean ever more conspicuously toward the biology side of that old debate over which more significantly determines one's nature: environment or genes, experiences or chromosomes.

Until a few years ago I couldn't account for my utter fascination with stone masons at work; whenever I encountered a rock wall going up, I would observe with the dedication other people give to a baseball game or a streetside watercolorist. When it came to spectatoring, I liked nothing more than watching a mortared or dry-laid wall rising piece by piece, the stone hammered to shape, the plumb line checked, the fitting, and then that final sweet laying into precise place a rock for the ages. When an opportunity at last came along for me to put up my own stone wall, I took up the labor to the exclusion of easier and much more lucrative work sitting before me. Native stone walls possessed me, and I long assumed the possession was just my idiosyncrasy, a thing I'd stumbled into on my own.

Then one Saturday afternoon I was roaming around a mostly forgotten corner of the Missouri Ozarks – ostensibly in search of information about a great-grandfather who came to this country in the mid-nineteenth century from the Yorkshire coast of northwest England, a man who wrote the first official state song of Missouri. I discovered that he was not simply my only ancestor to make a dollar now and then from writing, but he also was a mason who had worked his way westward from New York by laying up walls on the Erie Canal. Further questions turned up more: he apparently descended from men who for generations worked the semiprecious black stone commonly called jet found near Whitby, England. He was David Grayston, a surname I suspect may have derived from the mineral itself or the rock associated with it – a gray stone. The mystery opened at last: Why do I stand in near thrall to watch a stonemason at work? Because it's in my blood, my cells, the remotest part of me. Call it genetic memory.

Now I understand what happened years ago when I first wandered across an abandoned and hidden portion of the Illinois and Michigan Canal, where I stood transfixed by its simply dressed and still straight limestone lock walls: I was merely following the course of ancestral inclinings. I belonged to the canal in a way that only a recently recovered piece of my past could reveal. Today I wonder whether old Mr. Grayston, after working his way along the Erie Canal, did not continue his route by cutting and setting stone on the I&M and then following its southwesterly direction until it ran out – and all he could do then was stay the course it had set him on, until he arrived in the rocky country of the Ozarks, where he wrote lyrics, translated the Bible into couplets, and restored his clarity of mind by carving out limestone troughs and planters he sold from the back of an old wagon.

So, you see, I never had to learn to cherish the I&M Canal because my ancestry predestined it just as it did the color of my eyes or the curve of my lips. But I did have to learn the history of the canal; after all, knowledge does not (no matter how much a twelve-year-old learning the periodic table or the declension of a Latin noun might wish it) arrive in the blood (although a talent for Latin may). During those years I found it difficult getting to the story and exact route of the I&M because books and good maps were not readily available and many of the earliest sections of the waterway lay overgrown and hard to trace. Those circumstances, of course, made discovery all the more unexpected and exciting when it occurred.

All these things are the reasons I love *Prairie Passage* and the way research for it has helped reawaken and infuse an awareness of the canal and a concomitant desire in those who live close by to restore it and make it into a grand and shaping centerpiece of the first National Heritage Corridor in America. I've seen parts of the old waterway go from festering bogs of slime to lovely and evocative historical sites that are already driving economic changes and revivifying the towns and villages along its route. It's as if residents in the corridor have awakened from that oh-so-common American malaise of historical somnambulism and arisen to find new ways to remake an area. The old canal now is carrying us into a new country of the mind, where the freight is not coal but community.

Transport lies at the heart of American history: our economies, social ways, architecture, and – above all else – our sense of who we are and how we became who we are have been deeply and probably permanently shaped by the routes and means of traveling across this continent. Our past is a long chronicle of the ways we have continually devised – not always successfully – to connect ourselves, to link up into a topographic and political union, an arduous and, at times, seemingly impossible task, given our physiographic and cultural diversities.

The pioneer story – sometimes a myth, but always one of our most cherished lores – is ever so much about moving with the sun across the territory. The "Father of Our Country," George Washington, was himself a traveler and surveyor who, long before he became a general and a president, advocated and tried to build a canal from Chesapeake Bay across the Appalachians to the Ohio River. As much as we may worry about our children failing to learn basics, millions of them today can relate the story of Plymouth Rock, or recount a couple of details about Daniel Boone's indefatigable westering, or sing a few lines about that mule named Sal and her fifteen miles on the Erie Canal. We have entire organizations devoted to the preservation – historical and topographic – of the Santa Fe Trail, the Oregon and California Trail, the Mormon Trail; the ancient Natchez Trace has been reborn in almost its entire length as an aboundingly beautiful linear parkway through history. Beginning with our aboriginal peoples, Americans have perhaps the most peripatetic, the most moving history of any nation on Earth.

Now the time has come for the I&M to join these grand monuments in our national historical consciousness; the day is about to pass when I can mention the Illinois and Michigan Canal and hear a New Yorker or a Californian or a Texan ask out of enthusiastic perplexity, "How could a canal go from Illinois to Michigan? Isn't there a big lake in between?" The waterway from Lake Michigan to the Illinois River, our most westerly major transport canal, is, perhaps more than any other, the element, the force that turned Chicago from a village into our Second City. What the Erie Canal did for New York, the I&M did for the Prairie Metropolis, and this long-neglected waterway deserves a similar recognition.

The Illinois and Michigan Canal now promises to erase our forgetfulness and negligence, and to help halt some of the destruction of this huge and splendid cultural artifact. With books like *Prairie Passage* and the knowledge and passion it will generate, I believe Americans are ready to discover this magical resource, a thing we desperately need today: The more we use this canal and its rich history, the greater it becomes and the more of it there is for us to use.

NOTES ON MAPPING THE CORRIDOR

EDWARD RANNEY

For over twenty-five years I have dedicated my photographic work in large part to recording archaeological sites of ancient America. For some time I have hoped to bring this experience to bear in photographing both the midwestern landscape in which I grew up and the city in which I was born. In 1992 Gerald Adelmann, president of the Canal Corridor Association, unexpectedly offered me a commission to photograph the route of the Illinois and Michigan Canal, from Chicago to La Salle/Peru, enabling me to travel from my home in New Mexico to Chicago and explore in depth the multilayered historic landscape of the Illinois and Michigan Canal National Heritage Corridor.

The geography of my childhood is, by chance, connected on Illinois maps to the I&M Canal Corridor by a thin band of blue, the Des Plaines River, a slow-moving tributary of the Illinois River. As I photographed it south and west of the Chicago Portage site, I recalled wonderful childhood times canoeing and ice-skating, as well as special family gatherings at a small cabin owned by my grandparents, not far to the north, on that same Des Plaines River. These early experiences inform these landscape photographs as much as the sense of space formed by years of photographing Andean sites half a world away.

Certainly the legacy of my grandfather, Edward Ryerson, whose Des Plaines River property is now a unique Lake County Forest Preserve, connects me to this project in ways beyond the merely geographical. Awed by his reputation as a civic leader in Chicago, I felt closest to him when I watched him print his own pictures in his darkroom or listened to him explain the intricacies of the family tree he researched and meticulously drew. I was recently struck by a particular reminiscence in the family papers he preserved, one recorded in 1877 by his grandfather, Joseph T. Ryerson, recounting his arrival in Chicago, from Philadelphia, in 1842.

When I first arrived in Chicago, I was much disappointed, it had only 6600 people in it. . . . [E]verybody was poor, and it was a rather hard looking and appearing place, and I thought I could never stay in the town. . . . I soon became acquainted with a very good set of people – everyone seemed to have an independent, hearty way about them, spoke encouraging to me, and welcomed me. . . . Then I saw the streets were filled with teams drawing loads of wheat and farm produce from all directions, from one to two hundred miles that the store keepers were busy trading, and I made up my mind quickly that this was business; that Chicago must have some attraction and advantages, and was bound to grow and become an important city, and the longer I looked on and reasoned about it, the better I was pleased and satisfied, and it was not long before I became fascinated with the place and all about it, and its business prospects, so that no power could draw me away from it.

When I think of the places that drew me to invest this project with the sustained attention that would shape it into *Prairie Passage*, I think not only of the midwestern spaces of rivers, woodlands, and fields I grew up with but also of certain aspects of Chicago – the canyon-like feel of the river in the Loop, the always surprising vastness of Lake Michigan, the raw industrial landscape of south Chicago, and the unique sense of architectural space that characterizes the city itself. Places within the Canal Corridor now also hold a special resonance for me – the tangled growth of the Chicago Portage site, certain well-preserved, quiet sections of the I&M Canal near Morris, the few Native American habitation sites and burial mounds that have escaped desecration, and portions of Main Streets that ask for our attention and care. These, along with other places, stand as important reference points in the map of the corridor I came to carry in my head, a map more about a sense of space, collective memory, and the significance of place than about the literal, informative function of mapping.

For the first time in my work a limited number of aerial photographs have come to play a significant role in preparing a project for exhibition and publication. The aerials serve quite obviously as maps, orienting us as we follow the canal from the high density of metropolitan Chicago to the open space of the Illinois River valley. They serve too, perhaps, as metaphors for our movement through space and time and, like those nineteenth-century artistic renderings of towns and cities known as "balloon perspectives," provide vantage points that make the grids and patterns we have imposed on the landscape instantly understandable. The photographer Robert Adams has written that a primary function of landscape photography is to make intelligible to us what we already know. Certainly aerial photography shares this capacity. Though the aerial photograph distances us from its subject, at the same time it can give us a uniquely intimate sense

Figure 100. Edward Ryerson photographed this scene of family and friends on the Des Plaines River in 1928 on the property he acquired that year near Deerfield, Illinois, some fifty miles north of the Chicago Portage Site. (Courtesy of Edward Ranney.)

Figure 101. J. Carbutt made this ca. 1869 stereograph looking east toward the Chicago River and Lake Michigan from a vantage point above the Rush Street Bridge. (Courtesy of the Chicago Historical Society, ICHi 00166.)

of the interrelationships among the natural and the man-altered landscape.

From the moment I began to photograph in the Canal Corridor, I realized that historical images would provide very important references for this project. Drawings, engravings, and paintings have filled gaps where photographs were not available. It was not until around 1860, when photography's wet plate negative process became widely used in the United States, that photographic prints replaced the one-of-a-kind image produced by the daguerrotype or ambrotype. The greater sensibility and mobility of the wet plate negative process stimulated intense photographic activity not only in Chicago after 1860 but also along the western reaches of the I&M Canal. The albumen prints D. W. S. Rawson published in his 1866 album *The Valley of the Illinois* represent the most impressive early views of the Illinois River valley that have survived. The pictures of the canal near La Salle and of Peru's waterfront are excellent examples of the photographic technique that during this generation would document such important American events as the Civil War and the exploration and settlement of the West.

Rawson's former student and partner, W. E. Bowman, took over their joint studio in Ottawa in 1865 and quickly became the most widely known photographer in the area, both for his portrait work and for the popular series of stereographs he published on local towns and landscapes. James Jensen, who has studied Bowman's work in depth, has written that during the time Bowman was active, between 1857 and 1910, no fewer than forty-five other photographers are cited in newspaper accounts as working in Ottawa. A very small percentage of all this work, among which figure approximately fifty thousand glass plates by Bowman, has survived.

Important photographs of the Chicago River appeared around 1860, with work by A. J. W. Copelin followed by such evocative stereographs reproduced here as those by J. Carbutt and Lovejoy and Foster. Excellent pictures by John Gates, Fred Sonne, and Carl Ulrich, as well as the previously unpublished post–Chicago Fire landscape taken by the Civil War photographer George Barnard along the Chicago River, show distinctive changes along the downtown waterway and indicate the rich resources of original plates in the Chicago Architectural Photographing Co. archive. Equally important are the pictures by anonymous photographers selected from the vast archive of glass plates in the custody of the Metropolitan Water Reclamation District of Greater Chicago. The selection of views along the Chicago River and the documentation of the construction of the Sanitary and Ship Canal represent but a fraction of this rich, unstudied resource.

Lucy Lippard has written in *The Lure of the Local* (1997) that photographs are inherently "about memory" and that if it is "space that defines landscape, . . . [it] is space combined with memory that defines place." Each of the historical photographs in *Prairie Passage* contributes in its own way to re-creating a collective memory of the area. Yet none of the different bodies of work we have found, with the exception, perhaps, of the 1857 ambrotype of Chief Shabbona, evokes this memory as poignantly, I think, as the street scenes photographed by H. H. Carter. A pharmacist and amateur photographer, Carter used a hand-held camera to spontaneously capture the movement and expressions of his neighbors in downtown Lockport around 1915. The pictures are fascinating not just because they evoke a vanished time but because of Carter's sensitivity to a new kind of photographic image. The collection of 120 small glass plates taken by Carter have survived thanks to the concern of former Lockport resident Paul Ogren, who, since discovering them over forty-five years ago, has ensured their continued preservation.

Over the last twenty years landscape photographers have paid increasing attention to depicting the contemporary, man-altered landscape. Among the influences on this work are the writings of the late J. B. Jackson, one of the first in this country to focus his area of study exclusively on human geography and to insist, in his reading of the cultural landscape, on paying close attention to the vernacular elements in our lives that often go unnoticed. A central question Jackson's work raises – How can we value and preserve important historical aspects of the landscape yet simultaneously shape them to our present needs? – does seem to find some answers in the Illinois and Michigan Canal National Heritage Corridor. Certainly the Canal Corridor can be regarded now as one of those "zones of influence," which, in his introduction to *A Sense of Place, a Sense of Time* (1994), Jackson speculated could "nourish and hold a landscape together and provide it with instant accessibility."

Many people and institutions have played important roles in helping *Prairie Passage* to be realized, and I join with Emily Harris in extending warmest appreciation to them. My thanks also go to Emily herself, not only for her highly valued contributions to the text but also for coordinating innumerable details in the preparation of the book and exhibition and for greatly facilitating my work in the Canal Corridor. None of our undertakings would have been realized, of course, without the dedicated work of the Canal Corridor Association's founder and president for the last twenty years, Gerald Adelmann. I thank him warmly for the invitation to undertake this project and for his unstinting support and creative guidance as *Prairie Passage* grew to a scale and complexity not imagined in 1992.

Figure 102. This distinctive view of workers excavating the Sanitary and Ship Canal near Lockport in 1906 is from one of the many thousand glass plates preserved by the Metropolitan Water Reclamation District, Chicago. (Courtesy of the Metropolitan Water Reclamation District.)

BIBLIOGRAPHY

The following publications were consulted during the research for *Prairie Passage:*

Andreas, A. T. *History of Chicago.* Chicago: A. T. Andreas, 1884.

Baldwin, Elmer. *History of La Salle County, Illinois.* Chicago: Rand McNally and Co., 1877.

Balesi, Charles J. *The Time of the French in the Heart of North America, 1673–1818.* Chicago: Alliance Française, 1992.

Brown, Virginia Sparr, ed. *Grundy County Illinois Landmarks.* Rev. ed. Morris, Ill.: Grundy County Historical Society, 1997.

Buckingham, Joseph H. "Illinois as Lincoln Knew It: A Boston Reporter's Record of a Trip in 1847." *Illinois State Historical Society Transactions* (1937): 109–87.

Buisseret, David. *Historic Illinois from the Air.* Chicago: University of Chicago Press, 1990.

Cain, Louis P. *Sanitation Strategy for a Lakefront Metropolis: The Case of Chicago.* DeKalb: Northern Illinois University Press, 1978.

Chicago Department of Planning and Development, Commission on Chicago Landmarks. "I&M Canal Origins Site." Rev. report. Chicago, 1996.

Clemensen, A. Berle. *Illinois and Michigan Canal National Heritage Corridor: Historical Inventory, History, and Significance.* Denver: U.S. Department of the Interior, National Park Service, 1985.

Conzen, Michael P., ed. *Studies on the Illinois and Michigan Canal Corridor.* 8 vols. Committee on Geographical Studies. Chicago: University of Chicago, 1987–95.

Conzen, Michael P., and Kay J. Carr, eds. *Illinois and Michigan Canal National Heritage Corridor: A Guide to Its History and Sources.* DeKalb: Northern Illinois University Press, 1988.

Cronon, William. *Nature's Metropolis: Chicago and the Great West.* New York: W. W. Norton and Co., 1991.

Cunynghame, Sir Arthur. *A Glimpse at the Great Western Republic.* London: Bentley, 1851.

Federal Writers Project for the Works Progress Administration for the State of Illinois. *WPA Guide to Illinois.* Chicago: A. C. McClurg, 1939.

Garner, John S. *The Fitzpatrick Homestead: A University of Illinois Case Study in Recording Historic Buildings.* Champaign: School of Architecture, University of Illinois, 1987.

Jensen, James. "W. E. Bowman, General Photographer." Exhibition catalog. La Salle County Historical Society, Utica, Ill., 1979.

Heritage Conservation and Recreation Service. *Lockport, Illinois: An HCRS Project Report.* HCRS Publication No. 35. Washington, D.C.: U.S. Government Printing Office, 1980.

Historical Map and Guide to the Illinois and Michigan Canal National Heritage Corridor. Lockport, Ill.: Canal Corridor Association, 1993.

Howe, Walter A. *Documentary History of the Illinois and Michigan Canal: Legislation, Litigation, and Titles.* Springfield: State of Illinois, Department of Public Works and Buildings, 1956.

Hubbard, Gurdon S. *The Autobiography of Gurdon Saltonstall Hubbard: Pa-pa-ma-ta-be, "The Swift Walker."* 1888. Rpt., Chicago: R. R. Donnelley and Sons, 1981.

Lamb, John. *I&M Canal: A Corridor in Time.* Romeoville, Ill.: Lewis University, 1987.

Larson, John W. *Those Army Engineers: A History of the Chicago District, U.S. Army Corps of Engineers.* Washington, D.C.: U.S. Government Printing Office, 1980.

Legner, Linda. *Lockport, Illinois: A Collective Heritage.* Lockport, Ill.: Bank of Lockport, 1980.

Marseilles, Illinois, 1835–1985. Marseilles, Ill.: Marseilles 150, Inc., 1985.

Martineau, Harriet. *Society in America.* London: Saunders and Otley, 1837.

Mayer, Harold M., and Richard C. Wade. *Chicago: Growth of a Metropolis.* Chicago: University of Chicago Press, 1969.

Maze, Nancy C., ed. *Tales and Pictures of Peru, 1835–1985.* Peru, Ill.: N.p., 1985.

Miller, Donald L. *City of the Century: The Epic of Chicago and the Making of America.* New York: Simon and Schuster, 1996.

National Trust for Historic Preservation. *Regional Heritage Areas: Approaches to Sustainable Development.* Information Series No. 88. Washington, D.C., 1994.

Nattinger, E. A. "Nattinger's Souvenir of Ottawa Illinois in Nineteen Hundred. Complete Review." Ottawa, Ill.: E. A. Nattinger, 1900.

Pacyga, Dominic A., and Ellen Skerrett. *Chicago: City of Neighborhoods – Histories and Tours.* Chicago: Loyola University Press, 1986.

Peine, John D., and Debora A. Neurohr. *Illinois and Michigan Canal Corridor: A Concept Plan.* Ann Arbor, Mich.: U.S. Department of the Interior, National Park Service, 1981.

Putnam, James William. *The Illinois and Michigan Canal: A Study in Economic History.* Chicago: University of Chicago Press, 1918.

Rathbun, Mary Yeater. "The Illinois and Michigan Canal." Prepared for the Illinois Department of Conservation, Springfield, 1980.

Redd, Jim. *The Illinois and Michigan Canal: A Contemporary Perspective in Essays and Photographs.* Carbondale: Southern Illinois University Press, 1993.

Sandburg, Carl. *The Complete Poems of Carl Sandburg.* New York: Harcourt Brace Jovanovich, 1969.

The Story of Marseilles. Marseilles, Ill.: Marseilles Bicentennial Commission, 1976.

Sutton, Robert P., ed. *The Prairie State, Colonial Years to 1860: A Documentary History of Illinois.* Grand Rapids, Mich.: William B. Eerdmans, 1976.

Temple, Wayne C. *Lincoln's Connections with the Illinois and Michigan Canal.* Springfield: Illinois Bell, 1986.

Unonius, Gustaf. *A Pioneer in Northwest America, 1841–1858: The Memoirs of Gustaf Unonius.* 1950. Rpt., Trans. Jonas Oscar Backlund. Minneapolis: Swedish Pioneer Historical Society, 1960.

U.S. Department of the Interior, National Park Service. *An Inventory of Historic Engineering and Industrial Structures within the Illinois and Michigan Canal National Heritage Corridor.* Historic American Buildings Survey/Historic American Engineering Record. Washington, D.C., 1995.

——. *An Inventory of Historic Structures within the Illinois and Michigan Canal National Heritage Corridor.* 12 vols. Historic American Buildings Survey/Historic American Engineering Record. Washington, D.C., 1985.

Vierling, Philip E. *Hiking the Illinois and Michigan Canal and Exploring Its Environs.* Vol. 1: *La Salle to the Fox River.* Utica, Ill.: La Salle County Historical Society, 1986.

Way, Peter. *Common Labour: Workers and the Digging of North American Canals.* Cambridge: Cambridge University Press, 1993.

Wille, Lois. *Forever Open, Clear, and Free: The Historic Struggle for Chicago's Lakefront.* Chicago: Henry Regnery, 1972.

Also consulted were:

National Register of Historic Places. Nominations for various buildings and districts, available through the Illinois Historic Preservation Agency, Springfield, Ill., including:

American Steel and Wire Plant, Joliet
Coleman Hardware Building, Morris
Hegeler/Carus Mansion, La Salle
Hydroelectric Power Station, Marseilles
Lockport Historic District, Lockport
Sulphur Springs Hotel, La Salle County
Upper Bluff Historic District, Joliet

National Park Service brochures published by the Illinois and Michigan Canal National Heritage Corridor Commission, including:

"Archeology: Illinois and Michigan Canal National Heritage Corridor"
"Ice Age Geology: Illinois and Michigan Canal National Heritage Corridor"
"Illinois and Michigan Canal National Heritage Corridor"

In addition to the sources listed above, the Canal Corridor Association archives contributed valuable materials.

LIST OF PLATES, FIGURES, AND MAPS

PLATES

FIGURES

NOTES ON MAPPING THE CORRIDOR

MAPS